New

E AVAN B OLAND was bori ____ in 1967 and she has received numerous awards for her writing. She is Mabury Knapp Professor and Director of the Creative Writing Program at Stanford University. She divides her time between California and Dublin, where she lives with her husband, the novelist Kevin Casey.

EAVAN BOLAND

New Selected Poems

CARCANET

Acknowledgements

23 Poems was first published in 1962 by Gallagher Press, Dublin; *New Territory* in 1967 by Allen Figgis, Dublin; *The War Horse* in 1975 by Gollancz, London; *In Her Own Image* in 1980 by Arlen House, Dublin.

First published in Great Britain in 2013 by
Carcanet Press Limited
Alliance House
Cross Street
Manchester M2 7AQ

www.carcanet.co.uk

A CIP catalogue record for this book is available from the British Library

ISBN 978 1 84777 241 1

The publisher acknowledges financial assistance from Arts Council England

Typeset by XL Publishing Services, Exmouth
Printed and bound in England by SRP Ltd, Exeter

For Kevin, Sarah, Eavan and Éamonn

Contents

Author's Note   xiii

from New Territory   1967

Athene's Song   3
New Territory   4
From the Painting *Back from Market* by Chardin   5
Yeats in Civil War   6
Belfast vs Dublin   7

from The War Horse   1975

The War Horse   11
The Famine Road   12
Child of Our Time   13
Suburban Woman   14
The Laws of Love   17
O Fons Bandusiae   19
Cyclist with Cut Branches   20
Song   21

from In Her Own Image   1980

Anorexic   25
In Her Own Image   27
Making Up   28
Tirade for the Mimic Muse   30

from Night Feed   1982

Night Feed   35
Domestic Interior   36

Energies	37
Monotony	38
Endings	40
After a Childhood Away from Ireland	40
The Muse Mother	42
Woman in Kitchen	43
Patchwork or the Poet's Craft	44
Degas's Laundresses	45
It's a Woman's World	47
The New Pastoral	49
'Daphne with her thighs in bark'	50
The Woman Turns Herself into a Fish	52

from The Journey   1987

I

Self-Portrait on a Summer Evening	57
Mise Eire	59
The Oral Tradition	60
Fever	63
Lace	65
I Remember	66
The Bottle Garden	67
Suburban Woman: A Detail	68
The Briar Rose	70
The Women	70
Nocturne	72

II

The Journey	73
Envoi	77

III

Listen. This is the Noise of Myth	78
An Irish Childhood in England: 1951	81
Fond Memory	82
The Emigrant Irish	83
The Glass King	84

from Outside History 1990

I Object Lessons
    The Black Lace Fan My Mother Gave Me   89
    The Rooms of Other Women Poets   90
    The Shadow Doll   91
    The Latin Lesson   92
    Bright–Cut Irish Silver   93

II Outside History: A sequence
    I   The Achill Woman   95
    II   A False Spring   96
    III   The Making of an Irish Goddess   97
    IV   White Hawthorn in the West of Ireland   99
    V   Daphne Heard with Horror the Addresses of the God   100
    VI   The Photograph on My Father's Desk   101
    VII   We Are Human History. We Are Not Natural
      History.   102
    VIII   An Old Steel Engraving   103
    IX   In Exile   104
    X   We Are Always Too Late   105
    XI   What We Lost   106
    XII   Outside History   108

III Distances
    Distances   109
    Midnight Flowers   110
    Our Origins Are in the Sea   111
    What Love Intended   112

from In a Time of Violence 1994

The Singers   117

I Writing in a Time of Violence: A sequence
    1 That the Science of Cartography is Limited   118
    2 The Death of Reason   119

3 March 1 1847. By the First Post 120
4 In a Bad Light 121
5 The Dolls Museum in Dublin 123
6 Inscriptions 124
7 Beautiful Speech 126

II Legends
This Moment 128
Love 129
The Pomegranate 130
Moths 132
In Which the Ancient History I Learn Is Not My Own 133
The Parcel 135
Lava Cameo 137
Legends 138

III Anna Liffey
Anna Liffey 139
Time and Violence 146
A Woman Painted on a Leaf 148

from The Lost Land   1998

I Colony: A Sequence
1 My Country in Darkness 151
2 The Harbour 152
3 Witness 153
4 Daughters of Colony 154
5 Imago 155
6 The Scar 156
7 City of Shadows 157
8 Unheroic 158
9 The Colonists 160
10 A Dream of Colony 161
11 A Habitable Grief 162
12 The Mother Tongue 163

II The Lost Land
The Lost Land 165

Mother Ireland   166
The Blossom   168
Tree of Life   169
The Necessity for Irony   170
Heroic   171
Whose?   172

from Code   2001

I Marriage
   I In Which Hester Bateman, Eighteenth-Century English
      Silversmith, Takes an Irish Commission   175
   II Against Love Poetry   176
   III The Pinhole Camera   177
   IV Quarantine   178
   V Embers   179
   VI Then   180
   VII First Year   180
   VIII Once   182
   IX Thankëd be Fortune   183
   X A Marriage for the Millennium   184
   XI Lines for a Thirtieth Wedding Anniversary   185

II Code
   Code   186
   Limits   188
   Limits 2   188
   How We Made a New Art on Old Ground   189
   Making Money   191
   Exile! Exile!   193
   Is It Still the Same   194
   Irish Poetry   194

from Domestic Violence   2007

Domestic Violence
   1 Domestic Violence   199
   2 How the Dance Came to the City   201

3 How It Was Once In Our Country   202
4 Still Life   202
5 Silenced   204
6 Histories   205
7 Wisdom   205
8 Irish Interior   206
9 In Our Own Country   207

Letters to the Dead
An Elegy for my Mother In Which She Scarcely Appears   209
Amber   210
And Soul   211
On This Earth   213
Letters to the Dead   214
To Memory   215

Becoming the Hand of John Speed
Atlantis – A Lost Sonnet   217
Becoming the Hand of John Speed   218
Violence Against Women   219
Instructions   220
In Coming Days   221

New Poems

Art of Empire   225
The Long Evenings of their Leavetakings   226
Re-reading Oliver Goldsmith's 'Deserted Village' in a
    Changed Ireland   227
As   230
Becoming Anne Bradstreet   231
Cityscape   232
A Woman Without a Country   233

Index of First Lines   235
Index of Titles   239

Author's Note

This *New Selected* is unusual in one respect: it follows a *Collected Poems*, rather than preceding it. I have included poems from all of my previous volumes, beginning with *New Territory*, taking a broader sampling from some than from others. I have also included some new, as yet unpublished poems. In a small number of poems I have made minor adjustments to punctuation and layout compared with the previous versions.

Eavan Boland
Stanford/Dublin 2013

from NEW TERRITORY

1967

Athene's Song

for my father

From my father's head I sprung
Goddess of the war, created
Partisan and soldiers' physic –
My symbols boast and brazen gong –
Until I made in Athens wood
Upon my knees a new music.

When I played my pipe of bone,
Robbed and whittled from a stag,
Every bird became a lover
Every lover to its tone
Found the truth of song and brag;
Fish sprung in the full river.

Peace became the toy of power
When other noises broke my sleep.
Like dreams I saw the hot ranks
And heroes in another flower
Than any there; I dropped my pipe
Remembering their shouts, their thanks.

Beside the water, lost and mute,
Lies my pipe and like my mind
Remains unknown, remains unknown
And in some hollow taking part
With my heart against my hand
Holds its peace and holds its own.

New Territory

Several things announced the fact to us:
The captain's Spanish tears
Falling like doubloons in the headstrong light,
And then of course the fuss –
The crew jostling and interspersing cheers
With wagers. Overnight,
As we went down to our cabins, nursing the last
Of the grog, talking as usual of conquest,
Land hove into sight.

Frail compasses and trenchant constellations
Brought us as far as this,
And now air and water, fire and earth
Stand at their given stations
Out there, and are ready to replace
This single desperate width
Of ocean. Why do we hesitate? Water and air
And fire and earth and therefore life are here.
And therefore death.

Out of the dark man comes to life and into it
He goes and loves and dies,
(His element being the dark and not the light of day)
So the ambitious wit
Of poets and exploring ships have been his eyes –
Riding the dark for joy –
And so Isaiah of the sacred text is eagle-eyed because
By peering down the unlit centuries
He glimpsed the holy boy.

From the Painting Back from Market *by Chardin*

Dressed in the colours of a country day –
Grey-blue, blue-grey, the white of seagulls' bodies –
Chardin's peasant woman
Is to be found at all times in her short delay
Of dreams, her eyes mixed
Between love and market, empty flagons of wine
At her feet, bread under her arm. He has fixed
Her limbs in colour, and her heart in line.

In her right hand, the hindlegs of a hare
Peep from a cloth sack; through the door
Another woman moves
In painted daylight; nothing in this bare
Closet has been lost
Or changed. I think of what great art removes:
Hazard and death, the future and the past,
This woman's secret history and her loves –

And even the dawn market, from whose bargaining
She has just come back, where men and women
Congregate and go
Among the produce, learning to live from morning
To next day, linked
By a common impulse to survive, although
In surging light they are single and distinct,
Like birds in the accumulating snow.

Yeats in Civil War

Presently a strange thing happened:
I began to smell honey in places
where honey could not be.

In middle age you exchanged the sandals
Of a pilgrim for a Norman keep
In Galway. Civil war started, vandals
Sacked your country, made off with your sleep;

Somehow you arranged your escape
Aboard a spirit-ship which every day
Hoisted sail out of fire and rape.
On that ship your mind was stowaway.

The sun mounted on a wasted place,
But the wind at every door and turn
Blew the smell of honey in your face
Where there was none. Whatever we may learn

You are its sum, struggling to survive –
A fantasy of honey your reprieve.

Belfast vs Dublin

for Derek Mahon

Into this city of largesse
You carried clever discontent,
And now, the budget of your time here spent,
Let us not mince the word: this is no less
Than halfway towards the end. Gathering
In a rag tied to a stick, all in confusion,
Dublin reverence and Belfast irony –
Now hoist with your conclusion.

Cut by the throats before we spoke
One to another, yet we breast
The dour line of North and South, pressed
Into action by the clock. Here we renounce
All dividend except the brilliant quarrel
Of our towns: mine sports immoral
Courtiers in unholy waste, but your unwitty
Secret love for it is Belfast city.

We have had time to talk, and strongly
Disagree about the living out
Of life. There was no need to shout.
Rightly or else quite wrongly
We have run out of time, if not of talk.
Let us then cavalierly fork
Our ways, since we, and all unknown,
Have called into question one another's own.

from THE WAR HORSE

1975

The War Horse

This dry night, nothing unusual
About the clip, clop, casual

Iron of his shoes as he stamps death
Like a mint on the innocent coinage of earth.

I lift the window, watch the ambling feather
Of hock and fetlock, loosed from its daily tether

In the tinker camp on the Enniskerry Road,
Pass, his breath hissing, his snuffling head

Down. He is gone. No great harm is done.
Only a leaf of our laurel hedge is torn –

Of distant interest like a maimed limb,
Only a rose which now will never climb

The stone of our house, expendable, a mere
Line of defence against him, a volunteer

You might say, only a crocus its bulbous head
Blown from growth, one of the screamless dead.

But we, we are safe, our unformed fear
Of fierce commitment gone; why should we care

If a rose, a hedge, a crocus are uprooted
Like corpses, remote, crushed, mutilated?

He stumbles on like a rumour of war, huge,
Threatening; neighbours use the subterfuge

Of curtains; he stumbles down our short street
Thankfully passing us. I pause, wait,

Then to breathe relief lean on the sill
And for a second only my blood is still

With atavism. That rose he smashed frays
Ribboned across our hedge, recalling days

Of burned countryside, illicit braid:
A cause ruined before, a world betrayed.

The Famine Road

'Idle as trout in light Colonel Jones,
these Irish, give them no coins at all; their bones
need toil, their characters no less.' Trevelyan's
seal blooded the deal table. The Relief
Committee deliberated: 'Might it be safe,
Colonel, to give them roads, roads to force
from nowhere, going nowhere of course?'

> *'one out of every ten and then*
> *another third of those again*
> *women – in a case like yours.'*

Sick, directionless they worked; fork, stick
were iron years away; after all could
they not blood their knuckles on rock, suck
April hailstones for water and for food?
Why for that, cunning as housewives, each eyed –
as if at a corner butcher – the other's buttock.

> *'anything may have caused it, spores,*
> *a childhood accident; one sees*
> *day after day these mysteries.'*

Dusk: they will work tomorrow without him.
They know it and walk clear; he has become
a typhoid pariah, his blood tainted, although
he shares it with some there. No more than snow
attends its own flakes where they settle
and melt, will they pray by his death rattle.

> *'You never will, never you know*
> *but take it well woman, grow*
> *your garden, keep house, good-bye.'*

'It has gone better than we expected, Lord
Trevelyan, sedition, idleness, cured
in one; from parish to parish, field to field,
the wretches work till they are quite worn,
then fester by their work; we march the corn
to the ships in peace; this Tuesday I saw bones
out of my carriage window, your servant Jones.'

> *'Barren, never to know the load*
> *of his child in you, what is your body*
> *now if not a famine road ?'*

Child of Our Time

for Aengus

Yesterday I knew no lullaby
But you have taught me overnight to order
This song, which takes from your final cry
Its tune, from your unreasoned end its reason,
Its rhythm from the discord of your murder
Its motive from the fact you cannot listen.

We who should have known how to instruct
With rhymes for your waking, rhythms for your sleep,
Names for the animals you took to bed,
Tales to distract, legends to protect,
Later an idiom for you to keep
And living, learn, must learn from you, dead,

To make our broken images rebuild
Themselves around your limbs, your broken
Image, find for your sake whose life our idle
Talk has cost, a new language. Child
Of our time, our times have robbed your cradle.
Sleep in a world your final sleep has woken.

17 May 1974

Suburban Woman

I

Town and country at each other's throat –
between a space of truce until one night

walls began to multiply, to spawn
like lewd whispers of the goings-on,

the romperings, the rape on either side,
the smiling killing, that you were better dead

than let them get you. But they came, armed
with blades and ladders, with slimed

knives, day after day, week by week –
a proxy violation. She woke

one morning to the usual story: withdrawing,
neither side had gained, but there, dying,

caught in cross-fire, her past lay, bleeding
from wounds each meant for each, which needing

each other for other wars they could not inflict
one on another. Haemorrhaging to hacked

roads, in back gardens, like a pride
of lions toiled for booty, tribal acres died

and her world with them. She saw their power to sever
with a scar. She is the sole survivor.

II

Morning: mistress of talcums, spun
and second cottons, run tights
she is, courtesan to the lethal
rapine of routine. The room invites.
She reaches to fluoresce the dawn.
The kitchen lights like a brothel.

III

The chairs dusted and the morning
coffee break behind, she starts pawning

her day again to the curtains, the red
carpets, the stair rods, at last to the bed,

the unmade bed where once in an underworld
of limbs, her eyes freckling the night like jewelled

lights on a cave wall, she, crying, stilled,
bargained out of nothingness her child,

bartered from the dark her only daughter.
Waking, her cheeks dried, to a brighter

dawn she sensed in her as in April earth
a seed, a life ransoming her death.

IV

Late, quiet across her garden
sunlight shifts like a cat
burglar, thieving perspectives,
leaving her in the last light
alone, where, as shadows harden,
lengthen, silent she perceives
veteran dead-nettles, knapweed
crutched on walls, a summer's seed
of roses trenched in ramsons, and stares
at her life falling with her flowers,
like military tribute or the tears
of shell-shocked men, into arrears.

V

Her kitchen blind down – a white flag –
the day's assault over, now she will shrug

a hundred small surrenders off as images
stillborn, unwritten metaphors, blank pages

and on this territory, blindfold, we meet
at last, veterans of a defeat

no truce will heal, no formula prevent
breaking out fresh again; again the print

of twigs stalking her pillow will begin
a new day and all her victims then –

hopes unreprieved, hours taken hostage –
will newly wake, while I, on a new page

will watch, like town and country, word, thought
look for ascendancy, poise, retreat

leaving each line maimed, my forces used.
Defeated we survive, we two, housed

together in my compromise, my craft.
Who are of one another the first draft.

The Laws of Love

for Mary Robinson

At first light the legislator
Who schooled you, creator
Of each force, each element,
Its secret law, its small print
Nature – while dawn, baptismal as waters
Which broke early in dark, began –
First saw the first of your daughters
Become in your arms a citizen.

How easy for you to have made
For her a perfumed stockade,
How easy for you to impose
Laws and structures, torts for those
Fragments which matter less and less
As all fragments, and we must bless
The child, its murderer, defend
This chaos somehow which must end

With order. But who can separate
Hatred from its opposite
Or judge which is the other's source
Today, unless perhaps that force
Which makes your Moy in its ridge pool
Prime teenage trout for butchery,
While at the same time fulfil
The blood-tie of the tide, as we

Once new found sisters, each grown miser
With new found blood began to trade
Salmond for Shakespeare, none the wiser
Then but now I see it focus
Slowly a miracle, a closing wound.
That sisters kill, that sisters die, must mock us
Now, unless, with separate speech we find
For them new blood, for them now plead

Another world for whose horizons,
For whose anguish no reprieve
Exists unless new citizens,
And, as we found, laws of love –
We two whose very first worlds fell
Like wishes down a wishing well,
Ungranted, had we known, unwanted
Yet still there as the well is, haunted.

O Fons Bandusiae

Horace 3: XIII

Bold as crystal, bright as glass,
Your waters leap while we appear
Carrying to your woodland shrine
Gifts below your worthiness:
Grape and flower, Bandusia,
Yellow hawksbeard, ready wine.

And tomorrow we will bring
A struggling kid, his temples sore
With early horns, as sacrifice.
Tomorrow his new trumpeting
Will come to nothing, when his gore
Stains and thaws your bright ice.

Canicula, the lamp of drought,
The summer's fire, leaves your grace
Inviolate in the woods where
Every day you spring to comfort
The broad bull in his trace,
The herd out of the shepherd's care.

With every fountain, every spring
Of legend, I will set you down
In praise and immortal spate:
These waters which drop gossiping
To ground, this wet surrounding stone
And this green oak I celebrate.

Cyclist with Cut Branches

Country hands on the handlebars,
A bicycle bisecting cars
　　Lethal and casual
In rush hour traffic, I remember
Seeing, as I watched that September
　　For you as usual.

Like rapid mercury abused
By summer heat where it is housed
　　In slender telling glass,
My heart taking grief's temperature,
That summer, lost its powers to cure,
　　Its gift to analyse.

Jasmine and the hyacinth,
The lintel mortar and the plinth
　　Of spring across his bars,
Like globed grapes at first I thought,
Then at last more surely wrought
　　Like winter's single stars

Until I glimpsed not him but you
Like an animal the packs pursue
　　To covert in a forest,
And knew the branches were not spring's
Nor ever summer's ample things,
　　But decay's simple trust.

And since we had been like them cut
But from the flowering not the root
　　Then we had thanks to give –
That they and we had opened once,
Had found the light, had lost its glance
　　And still had lives to live.

Song

Where in blind files
Bats outsleep the frost
Water slips through stones
Too fast, too fast
For ice; afraid he'd slip
By me I asked him first.

Round as a bracelet
Clasping the wet grass,
An adder drowsed by berries
Which change blood to cess.
Dreading delay's venom
I risked the first kiss.

My skirt in my hand,
Lifting the hem high
I forded the river there.
Drops splashed my thigh.
Ahead of me at last
He turned at my cry:

'Look how the water comes
Boldly to my side;
See the waves attempt
What you have never tried.'
He late that night
Followed the leaping tide.

from IN HER OWN IMAGE

1980

Anorexic

Flesh is heretic.
My body is a witch.
I am burning it.

Yes I am torching
her curves and paps and wiles.
They scorch in my self denials.

How she meshed my head
in the half-truths
of her fevers

till I renounced
milk and honey
and the taste of lunch.

I vomited
her hungers.
Now the bitch is burning.

I am starved and curveless.
I am skin and bone.
She has learned her lesson.

Thin as a rib
I turn in sleep.
My dreams probe

a claustrophobia,
a sensuous enclosure.
How warm it was and wide

once by a warm drum,
once by the song of his breath
and in his sleeping side.

Only a little more,
only a few more days
sinless, foodless,

I will slip
back into him again
as if I had never been away.

Caged so
I will grow
angular and holy

past pain,
keeping his heart
such company

as will make me forget
in a small space
the fall

into forked dark,
into python needs
heaving to hips and breasts
and lips and heat
and sweat and fat and greed.

In Her Own Image

It is her eyes:
the irises are gold
and round they go
like the ring on my wedding finger,
round and round

and I can't touch
their histories or tears.
To think they were once my satellites!
They shut me out now.
Such light years!

She is not myself
anymore she is not
even in my sky
anymore and I
am not myself.

I will not disfigure
her pretty face.
Let her wear amethyst thumbprints,
a family heirloom,
a sort of burial necklace

and I know just the place:
Where the wall glooms,
where the lettuce seeds,
where the jasmine springs
no surprises

I will bed her.
She will bloom there,
second nature to me,
the one perfection
among compromises.

Making Up

My naked face;
I wake to it.
How it's dulsed and shrouded!
It's a cloud,

a dull pre-dawn.
But I'll soon
see to that.
I push the blusher up,

I raddle
and I prink,
pinking bone
till my eyes

are
a rouge-washed
flush on water.
Now the base

pales and wastes.
Light thins
from ear to chin,
whitening in

the ocean shine
mirror set
of my eyes
that I fledge

in old darks.
I grease and full
my mouth.
It won't stay shut:

I look
in the glass.
My face is made,
it says:

Take nothing, nothing
at its face value:
Legendary seas,
nakedness,

that up and stuck
lassitude
of thigh and buttock
that they prayed to –

it's a trick.
Myths
are made by men.
The truth of this

wave–raiding
sea–heaving
made–up
tale

of a face
from the source
of the morning
is my own:

Mine are the rouge pots,
the hot pinks,
the fledged
and edgy mix
of light and water
out of which
I dawn.

Tirade for the Mimic Muse

I've caught you out. You slut. You fat trout.
So here you are fumed in candle-stink.
Its yellow balm exhumes you for the glass.
How you arch and pout in it!
How you poach your face in it!
Anyone would think you were a whore –
An ageing out-of-work kind-hearted tart.
I know you for the ruthless bitch you are:
Our criminal, our tricoteuse, our Muse –
Our Muse of Mimic Art.

Eye-shadow, swivel brushes, blushers,
Hot pinks, rouge pots, sticks,
Ice for the pores, a mud mask –
All the latest tricks.
Not one of them disguise
That there's a dead millennium in your eyes.
You try to lamp the sockets of your loss:
The lives that famished for your look of love.
Your time is up. There's not a stroke, a flick
Can make your crime cosmetic.

With what drums and dances, what deceits
Rituals and flatteries of war,
Chants and pipes and witless empty rites
And war-like men
And wet-eyed patient women
You did protect yourself from horrors,
From the lizarding of eyelids
From the whiskering of nipples,
From the slow betrayals of our bedroom mirrors –
How you fled

The kitchen screw and the rack of labour,
The wash thumbed and the dish cracked,
The scream of beaten women,
The crime of babies battered,
The hubbub and the shriek of daily grief
That seeks asylum behind suburb walls –
A world you could have sheltered in your skirts –
And well I know and how I see it now,
The way you latched your belt and itched your hem
And shook it off like dirt.

And I who mazed my way to womanhood
Through all your halls of mirrors, making faces,
To think I waited on your trashy whim!
Hoping your lamp and flash,
Your glass, might show
This world I needed nothing else to know
But love and again love and again love.
In a nappy stink, by a soaking wash
Among stacked dishes
Your glass cracked,

Your luck ran out. Look. My words leap
Among your pinks, your stench pots and sticks.
They scatter shadow, swivel brushes, blushers.
Make your face naked.
Strip your mind naked.
Drench your skin in a woman's tears.
I will wake you from your sluttish sleep.
I will show you true reflections, terrors.
You are the Muse of all our mirrors.
Look in them and weep.

from NIGHT FEED

1982

Night Feed

This is dawn.
Believe me
This is your season, little daughter.
The moment daisies open,
The hour mercurial rainwater
Makes a mirror for sparrows.
It's time we drowned our sorrows.

I tiptoe in.
I lift you up
Wriggling
In your rosy, zipped sleeper.
Yes, this is the hour
For the early bird and me
When finder is keeper.

I crook the bottle.
How you suckle!
This is the best I can be,
Housewife
To this nursery
Where you hold on,
Dear life.

A silt of milk.
The last suck.
And now your eyes are open,
Birth-coloured and offended.
Earth wakes.
You go back to sleep.
The feed is ended.

Worms turn.
Stars go in.
Even the moon is losing face.
Poplars stilt for dawn
And we begin
The long fall from grace.
I tuck you in.

Domestic Interior

for Kevin

The woman is as round
as the new ring
ambering her finger.
The mirror weds her.
She has long since been bedded.

There is
about it all
a quiet search for attention
like the unexpected shine
of a despised utensil.

The oils,
the varnishes,
the cracked light,
the worm of permanence –
all of them supplied by Van Eyck –

by whose edict she will stay
burnished, fertile,
on her wedding day,
interred in her joy.
Love, turn.

The convex of your eye
that is so loving, bright
and constant yet shows
only this woman in her varnishes,
who won't improve in the light.

But there's a way of life
that is its own witness:
Put the kettle on, shut the blind.
Home is a sleeping child,
an open mind

and our effects,
shrugged and settled
in the sort of light
jugs and kettles
grow important by.

Energies

This is my time:
the twilight closing in,
a hissing on the ring,
stove noises, kettle steam
and children's kisses.

But the energy of flowers!
Their faces are so white –
my garden daisies –
they are so tight-fisted,
such economies of light.

In the dusk they have made hay:
in a banked radiance,
in an acreage of brightness
they are misering the day
while mine delays away

in chores left to do:
the soup, the bath, the fire
then bed-time,
up the stairs –
and there, there

the buttery curls,
the light,
the bran-fur of the teddy bear,
the fist like a night-time daisy,
damp and tight.

Monotony

The stilled hub
and polar drab
of the suburb
closes in.

In the round
of the staircase,
my arms sheafing nappies,
I grow in and down

to an old spiral,
a well of questions,
an oracle:
will it tell me

am I
at these altars,
warm shrines,
washing machines, dryers

with their incense
of men and infants,
priestess
or sacrifice?

My late tasks
wait like children:
milk bottles,
the milkman's note.

Cold air
clouds the rinsed,
milky glass,
blowing clear

with a hint
of winter constellations:
will I find
my answer where

Virgo reaps?
Her arms sheafing
the hemisphere,
hour after frigid hour,

her virgin stars,
her maidenhead
married to force
harry us

to wed our gleams
to brute routines:
solstices,
small families.

Endings

A child
shifts in a cot.
No matter what happens now
I'll never fill one again.

It's a night
white things ember in:
jasmine and the shine –
flowering, opaline –
of the apple trees.

If I lean
I can see
what it is the branches end in:

The leaf.
The reach.
The blossom.
The abandon.

After a Childhood Away from Ireland

One summer
we slipped in at dawn
on plum-coloured water
in the sloppy quiet.

The engines
of the ship stopped.
There was an eerie
drawing near,

a noiseless coming head-on
of red roofs, walls,
dogs, barley stooks.
Then we were there.

Cobh.
Coming home.
I had heard of this:
the ground the emigrants

resistless, weeping
laid their cheeks to,
put their lips to kiss.
Love is also memory.

I only stared.
What I had lost
was not land
but the habit of land:

whether of growing out of
or settling back on,
or being
defined by.

I climb
to your nursery.
I stand listening
to the dissonances

of the summer's day ending.
I bend to kiss you.
Your cheeks
are brick pink.

The Muse Mother

My window pearls wet.
The bare rowan tree
berries rain.

I can see
from where I stand
a woman hunkering –
her busy hand
worrying a child's face,

working a nappy liner
over his sticky loud
round of a mouth.

Her hand's a cloud
across his face
making light and rain,
smiles and a frown,
a smile again.

She jockeys him to her hip,
pockets the nappy liner,
collars rain on her nape
and moves away

but my mind stays fixed:

if I could only decline her –
lost noun
out of context,
stray figure of speech –
from this rainy street

again to her roots,
she might teach me
a new language:

to be a sibyl
able to sing the past
in pure syllables,
limning hymns sung
to belly wheat or a woman –

able to speak at last
my mother tongue.

Woman in Kitchen

Breakfast over, islanded by noise,
she watches the machines go fast and slow.
She stands among them as they shake the house.
They move. Their destination is specific.
She has nowhere definite to go:
she might be a pedestrian in traffic.

White surfaces retract. White
sideboards light the white of walls.
Cups wink white in their saucers.
The light of day bleaches as it falls
on cups and sideboards. She could use
the room to tap with if she lost her sight.

Machines jigsaw everything she knows.
And she is everywhere among their furor:
the tropic of the dryer tumbling clothes.
The round lunar window of the washer.
The kettle in the toaster is a kingfisher
swooping for trout above the river's mirror.

The wash done, the kettle boiled, the sheets
spun and clean, the dryer stops dead.
The silence is a death. It starts to bury
the room in white spaces. She turns to spread
a cloth on the board and irons sheets
in a room white and quiet as a mortuary.

Patchwork or the Poet's Craft

I have been thinking at random
on the universe
or rather, how nothing in the universe
is random –

(there's nothing like presumption late at night.)

My sumptuous
trash bag of colours –
Laura Ashley cottons –
waits to be cut
and stitched and patched

but there's a mechanical feel
about the handle
of my second-hand sewing machine,
with its flowers
and *Singer* painted orange on it.
And its iron wheel.

My back is to the dark.
Somewhere out there
are stars and bits of stars
and little bits of bits.
And swiftnesses and brightnesses and drift.

But is it craft or art?

I will be here
till midnight,
cross-legged in the dining-room,
logging triangles and diamonds,
cutting and aligning,
finding greens in pinks
and burgundies in whites
until I finish it.

There's no reason in it.

Only when it's laid
right across the floor,
sphere on square
and seam on seam,
in a good light –
a night-sky spread –
will it start to hit me.

These are not bits.
They are pieces.
And the pieces fit.

Degas's Laundresses

You rise, you dawn
roll-sleeved Aphrodites,
out of a camisole brine,
a linen pit of stitches,
silking the fitted sheets
away from you like waves.

You seam dreams in the folds
of wash from which freshes
the whiff and reach of fields
where it bleached and stiffened.
Your chat's sabbatical:
brides, wedding outfits,

a pleasure of leisured women
are sweated into the folds,
the neat heaps of linen.
Now the drag of the clasp.
Your wrists basket your waist.
You round to the square weight.

Wait. There behind you.
A man. There behind you.
Whatever you do don't turn.
Why is he watching you?
Whatever you do don't turn.
Whatever you do don't turn.

See he takes his ease
staking his easel so,
slowly sharpening charcoal,
closing his eyes just so,
slowly smiling as if
so slowly he is

unbandaging his mind.
Surely a good laundress
would understand its twists,
its white turns,
its blind designs –

it's your winding sheet.

It's a Woman's World

Our way of life
has hardly changed
since a wheel first
whetted a knife.

Maybe flame
burns more greedily
and wheels are steadier
but we're the same

who milestone
our lives
with oversights –
living by the lights

of the loaf left
by the cash register,
the washing powder
paid for and wrapped,

the wash left wet:
like most historic peoples
we are defined
by what we forget,

by what we will never be –
star-gazers,
fire-eaters.
It's our alibi

for all time:
as far as history goes
we were never
on the scene of the crime.

So when the king's head
gored its basket –
grim harvest –
we were gristing bread

or getting the recipe
for a good soup
to appetise
our gossip.

It's still the same.
By night our windows
moth our children
to the flame

of hearth not history.
And still no page
scores the low music
of our outrage.

Appearances
still reassure:
that woman there
craned to the starry mystery

is merely getting a breath
of evening air,
while this one here –
her mouth

a burning plume –
she's no fire-eater,
just my frosty neighbour
coming home.

The New Pastoral

The first man had flint to spark. He had a wheel
to read his world

I'm in the dark.

I am a lost, last inhabitant –
displaced person
in a pastoral chaos.

All day I listen to
the loud distress, the switch and tick of
new herds.

But I'm no shepherdess.

Can I unbruise these sprouts or clean this mud flesh
till it roots again?
Can I make whole
this lamb's knuckle, butchered from its last crooked suckling?

I could be happy here,
I could be something more than a refugee

were it not for this lamb unsuckled, for the nonstop
switch and tick
telling me

there was a past,
there was a pastoral,
and these chance sights

what are they all
but amnesias of a rite

I danced once on a frieze?

'Daphne with her thighs in bark'

I have written this

so that,
in the next myth,
my sister will be wiser.

Let her learn from me:

the opposite of passion
is not virtue
but routine.

Look at me

I can be cooking,
making coffee,
scrubbing wood, perhaps,
and back it comes:
the crystalline, the otherwhere,
the wood

where I was
when he began the chase.
And how I ran from him!

Pan-thighed,
satyr-faced he was.

The trees reached out to me.
I silvered and
I quivered. I shook out
my foil of quick leaves.

He snouted past.
What a fool I was!

I shall be here forever,
setting out the tea,
among the coppers and the branching alloys and
the tin shine of this kitchen;
laying saucers on the pine table.

Save face, sister.
Fall. Stumble.
Rut with him.
His rough heat will keep you warm and

you will be better off than me,
with your memories
down the garden,
at the start of March,

unable to keep your eyes
off the chestnut tree –

just the way
it thrusts and hardens

The Woman Turns Herself into a Fish

Unpod
the bag,
the seed.

Slap
the flanks back.
Flatten

paps.
Make finny
scaled

and chill
the slack
and dimple

of the rump.
Pout
the mouth,

brow the eyes
and now
and now

eclipse
in these hips,
these loins

the moon,
the blood
flux.

It's done.
I turn,
I flab upward

blub-lipped,
hipless
and I am

sexless
shed
of ecstasy,

a pale
swimmer
sequin-skinned,

pearling eggs
screamlessly
in seaweed.

It's what
I set my heart on.
Yet

ruddering
and muscling
in the sunless tons

of new freedoms,
still
I feel

a chill pull,
a brightening,
a light, a light,

and how
in my loomy cold,
my greens,

still
she moons
in me.

from THE JOURNEY

1987

I

Self-Portrait on a Summer Evening

Jean-Baptiste Chardin
is painting a woman
in the last summer light.

All summer long
he has been slighting her
in botched blues, tints
half-tones, rinsed neutrals.

What you are watching
is light unlearning itself
an infinite unfrocking of the prism.

Before your eyes
the ordinary life
is being glazed over:
pigments of the bibelot
the cabochon, the water-opal
pearl to the intimate
simple colours of
her ankle-length summer skirt.

Truth makes shift:
the triptych shrinks
to the cabinet picture.

Can't you feel it?
Aren't you chilled by it?
The way the late afternoon
is reduced to detail –

the sky that odd shape of apron –

opaque, scumbled –
the lazulis of the horizon becoming

optical greys
before your eyes
before your eyes
in my ankle-length
summer skirt

crossing between
the garden and the house,
under the whitebeam trees,
keeping an eye on
the length of the grass,
the height of the hedge,
the distance of the children

I am Chardin's woman

edged in reflected light,
hardened by
the need to be ordinary.

Mise Eire

I won't go back to it –

my nation displaced
into old dactyls,
oaths made
by the animal tallows
of the candle –

land of the Gulf Stream,
the small farm,
the scalded memory,
the songs
that bandage up the history,
the words
that make a rhythm of the crime

where time is time past.
A palsy of regrets.
No. I won't go back.
My roots are brutal:

I am the woman –
a sloven's mix
of silk at the wrists,
a sort of dove-strut
in the precincts of the garrison –

who practises
the quick frictions,
the rictus of delight
and gets cambric for it,
rice-coloured silks.

I am the woman
in the gansy-coat
on board the *Mary Belle*,
in the huddling cold,

holding her half-dead baby to her
as the wind shifts east
and north over the dirty
water of the wharf

mingling the immigrant
guttural with the vowels
of homesickness who neither
knows nor cares that

a new language
is a kind of scar
and heals after a while
into a passable imitation
of what went before.

The Oral Tradition

I was standing there
at the end of a reading
or a workshop or whatever,
watching people heading
out into the weather,

only half-wondering
what becomes of words,
the brisk herbs of language,
the fragrances we think we sing,
if anything.

We were left behind
in a firelit room
in which the colour scheme
crouched well down –
golds, a sort of dun

a distressed ochre –
and the sole richness was
in the suggestion of a texture
like the low flax gleam
that comes off polished leather.

Two women
were standing in shadow,
one with her back turned.
Their talk was a gesture,
an outstretched hand.

They talked to each other
and words like 'summer'
'birth' 'great-grandmother'
kept pleading with me,
urging me to follow.

'She could feel it coming' –
one of them was saying –
'all the way there,
across the fields at evening
and no one there, God help her

'and she had on a skirt
of cross-woven linen
and the little one
kept pulling at it.
It was nearly night ...'

(Wood hissed and split
in the open grate,
broke apart in sparks,
a windfall of light
in the room's darkness)

'… when she lay down
and gave birth to him
in an open meadow.
What a child that was
to be born without a blemish!'

It had started raining,
the windows dripping, misted.
One moment I was standing
not seeing out,
only half-listening

staring at the night; the next
without warning
I was caught by it:
the bruised summer light,
the musical sub-text

of mauve eaves on lilac
and the laburnum past
and shadow where the lime
tree dropped its bracts
in frills of contrast

where she lay down
in vetch and linen
and lifted up her son
to the archive
they would shelter in:

the oral song
avid as superstition,
layered like an amber in
the wreck of language
and the remnants of a nation.

I was getting out
my coat, buttoning it,
shrugging up the collar.
It was bitter outside,
a real winter's night

and I had distances
ahead of me: iron miles
in trains, iron rails
repeating instances
and reasons; the wheels

singing innuendoes, hints,
outlines underneath
the surface, a sense
suddenly of truth,
its resonance.

Fever

is what remained or what they thought
remained after the ague and the sweats
were over and the shock of wild flowers
at the bedside had been taken away;

is what they tried to shake out of
the crush and dimple of cotton,
the shy dust of a bridal skirt;
is what they beat, lashed, hurt like

flesh as if it were a lack of virtue
in a young girl sobbing her heart out
in a small town for having been seen
kissing by the river; is what they burned

alive in their own back gardens
as if it were a witch and not the full-
length winter gaberdine and breathed again
when the fires went out in charred dew.

My grandmother died in a fever ward,
younger than I am and far from
the sweet chills of a Louth spring –
its sprigged light and its wild flowers –

with five orphan daughters to her name.
Names, shadows, visitations, hints
and a half-sense of half-lives remain.
And nothing else, nothing more unless

I re-construct the soaked-through midnights;
vigils; the histories I never learned
to predict the lyric of; and re-construct
risk; as if silence could become rage,

as if what we lost is a contagion
that breaks out in what cannot be
shaken out from words or beaten out
from meaning and survives to weaken

what is given, what is certain
and burns away everything but this
exact moment of delirium when
someone cries out someone's name.

Lace

Bent over
the open notebook –

light fades out
making the trees stand out
and my room
at the back
of the house, dark.

In the dusk
I am still
looking for it –
the language that is

lace:

a baroque obligation
at the wrist
of a prince
in a petty court.
Look, just look
at the way he shakes out

the thriftless phrases,
the crystal rhetoric
of bobbined knots
and bosses:
a vagrant drift
of emphasis
to wave away an argument
or frame the hand
he kisses;
which, for all that, is still

what someone
in the corner
of a room,
in the dusk,
bent over
as the light was fading

lost their sight for.

I Remember

I remember the way the big windows washed
out the room and the winter darks tinted
it and how, in the brute quiet and aftermath,
an eyebrow waited helplessly to be composed

from the palette with its scarabs of oil
colours gleaming through a dusk leaking from
the iron railings and the ruined evenings of
bombed-out, post-war London; how the easel was

mulberry wood and, porcupining in a jar,
the spines of my mother's portrait brushes
spiked from the dirty turpentine and the face
on the canvas was the scattered fractions

of the face which had come up the stairs
that morning and had taken up position in
the big drawing-room and had been still
and was now gone; and I remember, I remember

I was the interloper who knows both love and fear,
who comes near and draws back, who feels nothing
beyond the need to touch, to handle, to dismantle it,
the mystery; and how in the morning when I came down –

a nine-year-old in high, fawn socks –
the room had been shocked into a glacier
of cotton sheets thrown over the almond
and vanilla silk of the French Empire chairs.

The Bottle Garden

I decanted them – feather mosses, fan-shaped plants,
asymmetric greys in the begonia –
into this globe which shows up how the fern shares
the invertebrate lace of the sea-horse.

The sun is in the bottle garden,
submarine, out of its element
when I come down on a spring morning;
my sweet, greenish, inland underwater.

And in my late thirties, past the middle way,
I can say how did I get here?
I hardly know the way back, still less forward.
Still, if you look for them, there are signs:

Earth stars, rock spleenwort, creeping fig
and English ivy all furled and herded
into the green and cellar wet
of the bottle; well, here they are

here I am a gangling schoolgirl
in the convent library, the April evening outside,
reading the *Aeneid* as the room darkens
to the underworld of the Sixth Book –

the Styx, the damned, the pity and
the improvised poetic of imprisoned meanings;
only half aware of the open weave of harbour lights
and my school blouse riding up at the sleeves.

Suburban Woman: A Detail

I

The chimneys have been swept.
The gardens have their winter cut.
The shrubs are prinked, the hedges gelded.

The last dark shows up the headlights
of the cars coming down the Dublin mountains.

Our children used to think they were stars.

II

This is not the season
when the goddess rose
out of seed, out of wheat,
out of thawed water
and went, distracted and astray,
to find her daughter.

Winter will be soon:
dun pools of rain;
ruddy, addled distances;
winter pinks, tinges and
a first-thing smell of turf
when I take the milk in.

III

Setting out for a neighbour's house
in a denim skirt,

a blouse blended in
by the last light,

I am definite
to start with
but the light is lessening,
the hedge losing its detail,
the path its edge.

Look at me, says the tree.
I was a woman once like you,
full-skirted, human.

Suddenly I am not certain
of the way I came
or the way I will return,
only that something
which may be nothing
more than darkness has begun
softening the definitions
of my body, leaving

the fears and all the terrors
of the flesh shifting the airs
and forms of the autumn quiet

crying 'remember us'.

The Briar Rose

Intimate as underthings
beside the matronly damasks –

the last thing
to go out at night
is the lantern-like, white insistence
of these small flowers;

their camisole glow.

Standing here on the front step
watching wildness break out again

it could be
the unlighted stairway,
I could be
the child I was, opening

a bedroom door
on Irish whiskey, lipstick,
an empty glass,
oyster crêpe-de-Chine

and closing it without knowing why.

The Women

This is the hour I love: the in-between,
neither here-nor-there hour of evening.
The air is tea-coloured in the garden.
The briar rose is spilled crêpe-de-Chine.

This is the time I do my work best,
going up the stairs in two minds,
in two worlds, carrying cloth or glass,
leaving something behind, bringing
something with me I should have left behind.

The hour of change, of metamorphosis,
of shape-shifting instabilities.
My time of sixth sense and second sight
when in the words I choose, the lines I write,
they rise like visions and appear to me:

women of work, of leisure, of the night,
in stove-coloured silks, in lace, in nothing,
with crewel needles, with books, with wide open legs

who fled the hot breath of the god pursuing,
who ran from the split hoof and the thick lips
and fell and grieved and healed into myth,

into me in the evening at my desk
testing the water with a sweet quartet,
the physical force of a dissonance –

the fission of music into syllabic heat –
and getting sick of it and standing up
and going downstairs in the last brightness

into a landscape without emphasis,
light, linear, precisely planned,
a hemisphere of tiered, aired cotton,

a hot terrain of linen from the iron
folded in and over, stacked high
neatened flat, stoving heat and white.

Nocturne

After a friend has gone I like the feel of it:
the house at night. Everyone asleep.
The way it draws in like atmosphere or evening.

One o'clock. A floral teapot and a raisin scone.
A tray waits to be taken down.
The landing light is off. The clock strikes. The cat

comes into his own, mysterious on the stairs,
a black ambivalence around the legs of button-back
chairs, an insinuation to be set beside

the red spoon and the salt-glazed cup,
the saucer with the thick spill of tea
which scalds off easily under the tap. Time

is a tick, a purr, a drop. The spider
on the dining room window has fallen asleep
among complexities as I will once

the doors are bolted and the keys tested
and the switch turned up of the kitchen light
which made outside in the back garden

an electric room – a domestication
of closed daisies, an architecture
instant and improbable.

II

The Journey

for Elizabeth Ryle

*Immediately cries were heard. These were the loud wailing of infant souls weeping
at the very entrance-way; never had they had their share of life's sweetness for
the dark day had stolen them from their mothers' breasts and plunged them
to a death before their time.*

Virgil, The Aeneid, *Book VI*

And then the dark fell and 'there has never'
I said 'been a poem to an antibiotic:
never a word to compare with the odes on
the flower of the raw sloe for fever

'or the devious Africa-seeking tern
or the protein treasures of the sea-bed.
Depend on it, somewhere a poet is wasting
his sweet uncluttered metres on the obvious

'emblem instead of the real thing.
Instead of sulpha we shall have hyssop dipped
in the wild blood of the unblemished lamb,
so every day the language gets less

'for the task and we are less with the language.'
I finished speaking and the anger faded
and dark fell and the book beside me
lay open at the page Aphrodite

comforts Sappho in her love's duress.
The poplars shifted their music in the garden,
a child startled in a dream,
my room was a mess –

the usual hardcovers, half-finished cups,
clothes piled up on an old chair –
and I was listening out but in my head was
a loosening and sweetening heaviness,

not sleep, but nearly sleep, not dreaming really
but as ready to believe and still
unfevered, calm and unsurprised
when she came and stood beside me

and I would have known her anywhere
and I would have gone with her anywhere
and she came wordlessly
and without a word I went with her

down down down without so much as
ever touching down but always, always
with a sense of mulch beneath us
the way of stairs winding down to a river

and as we went on the light went on
failing and I looked sideways to be certain
it was she, misshapen, musical –
Sappho – the scholiast's nightingale

and down we went, again down
until we came to a sudden rest
beside a river in what seemed to be
an oppressive suburb of the dawn.

My eyes got slowly used to the bad light.
At first I saw shadows, only shadows.
Then I could make out women and children
and, in the way they were, the grace of love.

'Cholera, typhus, croup, diphtheria'
she said, 'in those days they racketed
in every backstreet and alley of old Europe.
Behold the children of the plague.'

Then to my horror I could see to each
nipple some had clipped a limpet shape –
suckling darknesses – while others had their arms
weighed down, making terrible pietàs.

She took my sleeve and said to me, 'be careful.
Do not define these women by their work:
not as washerwomen trussed in dust and sweating,
muscling water into linen by the river's edge

'nor as court ladies brailled in silk
on wool and woven with an ivory unicorn
and hung, nor as laundresses tossing cotton,
brisking daylight with lavender and gossip.

'But these are women who went out like you
when dusk became a dark sweet with leaves,
recovering the day, stooping, picking up
teddy bears and rag dolls and tricycles and buckets –

'love's archaeology – and they too like you
stood boot deep in flowers once in summer
or saw winter come in with a single magpie
in a caul of haws, a solo harlequin.'

I stood fixed. I could not reach or speak to them.
Between us was the melancholy river,
the dream water, the narcotic crossing
and they had passed over it, its cold persuasions.

I whispered, 'let me be
let me at least be their witness,' but she said
'what you have seen is beyond speech,
beyond song, only not beyond love;

'remember it, you will remember it'
and I heard her say but she was fading fast
as we emerged under the stars of heaven,
'there are not many of us; you are dear

'and stand beside me as my own daughter.
I have brought you here so you will know forever
the silences in which are our beginnings,
in which we have an origin like water,'

and the wind shifted and the window clasp
opened, banged and I woke up to find
the poetry books stacked higgledy piggledy,
my skirt spread out where I had laid it;

nothing was changed; nothing was more clear
but it was wet and the year was late.
The rain was grief in arrears; my children
slept the last dark out safely and I wept.

Envoi

It is Easter in the suburb. Clematis
shrubs the eaves and trellises with pastel.
The evenings lengthen and before the rain
the Dublin mountains become visible.

My muse must be better than those of men
who made theirs in the image of their myth.
The work is half-finished and I have nothing
but the crudest measures to complete it with.

Under the street-lamps the dustbins brighten.
The winter flowering jasmine casts a shadow
outside my window in my neighbour's garden.
These are the things that my muse must know.

She must come to me. Let her come
to be among the donnée, the given.
I need her to remain with me until
the day is over and the song is proven.

Surely she comes, surely she comes to me –
no lizard skin, no paps, no podded womb
about her but a brightening and
the consequences of an April tomb.

What I have done I have done alone.
What I have seen is unverified.
I have the truth and I need the faith.
It is time I put my hand in her side.

If she will not bless the ordinary,
if she will not sanctify the common,
then here I am and here I stay and then am I
the most miserable of women.

III

Listen. This is the Noise of Myth

This is the story of a man and woman
under a willow and beside a weir
near a river in a wooded clearing.
They are fugitives. Intimates of myth.

Fictions of my purpose. I suppose
I shouldn't say that yet or at least
before I break their hearts or save their lives
I ought to tell their story and I will.

When they went first it was winter; cold,
cold through the Midlands and as far West
as they could go. They knew they had to go –
through Meath, Westmeath, Longford,

their lives unravelling like the hours of light –
and then there were lambs under the snow
and it was January, aconite and jasmine
and the hazel yellowing and puce berries on the ivy.

They could not eat where they had cooked,
nor sleep where they had eaten
nor at dawn rest where they had slept.
They shunned the densities

of trees with one trunk and of caves
with one dark and the dangerous embrace
of islands with a single landing place.
And all the time it was cold, cold:

the fields still gardened by their ice,
the trees stitched with snow overnight,
the ditches full; frost toughening lichen,
darning lace into rock crevices.

And then the woods flooded and buds
blunted from the chestnut and the foxglove
put its big leaves out and chaffinches
chinked and flirted in the branches of the ash.

And here we are where we started from –
under a willow and beside a weir
near a river in a wooded clearing.
The woman and the man have come to rest.

Look how light is coming through the ash.
The weir sluices kingfisher blues.
The woman and the willow tree lean forward, forward.
Something is near; something is about to happen;

something more than spring
and less than history. Will we see
hungers eased after months of hiding?
Is there a touch of heat in that light?

If they stay here soon it will be summer; things
returning, sunlight fingering minnowy deeps,
seedy greens, reeds, electing lights
and edges from the river. Consider

legend, self-deception, sin, the sum
of human purpose and its end; remember
how our poetry depends on distance,
aspect: gravity will bend starlight.

Forgive me if I set the truth to rights.
Bear with me if I put an end to this:
She never turned to him; she never leaned
under the sallow-willow over to him.

They never made love; not there; not here;
not anywhere; there was no winter journey;
no aconite, no birdsong and no jasmine,
no woodland and no river and no weir.

Listen. This is the noise of myth. It makes
the same sound as shadow. Can you hear it?
Daylight greys in the preceptories.
Her head begins to shine

pivoting the planets of a harsh nativity.
They were never mine. This is mine.
This sequence of evicted possibilities.
Displaced facts. Tricks of light. Reflections.

Invention. Legend. Myth. What you will.
The shifts and fluencies are infinite.
The moving parts are marvellous. Consider
how the bereavements of the definite

are easily lifted from our heroine.
She may or she may not. She was or wasn't
by the water at his side as dark
waited above the Western countryside.

O consolations of the craft.
How we put
the old poultices on the old sores,
the same mirrors to the old magic. Look.

The scene returns. The willow sees itself
drowning in the weir and the woman
gives the kiss of myth her human heat.
Reflections. Reflections. He becomes her lover.

The old romances make no bones about it.
The long and short of it. The end and the beginning.
The glories and the ornaments are muted.
And when the story ends the song is over.

An Irish Childhood in England: 1951

The bickering of vowels on the buses,
the clicking thumbs and the big hips of
the navy-skirted ticket collectors with
their crooked seams brought it home to me:
Exile. Ration-book pudding.
Bowls of dripping and the fixed smile
of the school pianist playing 'Iolanthe',
'Land of Hope and Glory' and 'John Peel'.

I didn't know what to hold, to keep.
At night, filled with some malaise
of love for what I'd never known I had,
I fell asleep and let the moment pass.
The passing moment has become a night
of clipped shadows, freshly painted houses,
the garden eddying in dark and heat,
my children half-awake, half-asleep.

Airless, humid dark. Leaf-noise.
The stirrings of a garden before rain.
A hint of storm behind the risen moon.
We are what we have chosen. Did I choose to –
in a strange city, in another country,
on nights in a north-facing bedroom,
waiting for the sleep that never did
restore me as I'd hoped to what I'd lost –

let the world I knew become the space
between the words that I had by heart
and all the other speech that always was
becoming the language of the country that
I came to in nineteen-fifty-one? –
barely-gelled, a freckled six-year-old,
overdressed and sick on the plane
when all of England to an Irish child

was nothing more than what you'd lost and how:
was the teacher in the London convent who
when I produced 'I amn't' in the classroom
turned and said – 'you're not in Ireland now'.

Fond Memory

It was a school where all the children wore darned worsted;
where they cried – or almost all – when the Reverend Mother
announced at lunch-time that the King had died

peacefully in his sleep. I dressed in wool as well,
ate rationed food, played English games and learned
how wise the Magna Carta was, how hard the Hanoverians

had tried, the measure and complexity of verse,
the hum and score of the whole orchestra.
At three o'clock I caught two buses home

where sometimes in the late afternoon
at a piano pushed into a corner of the playroom
my father would sit down and play the slow

lilts of Tom Moore while I stood there trying
not to weep at the cigarette smoke stinging up
from between his fingers and – as much as I could think –

I thought this is my country, was, will be again,
this upward-straining song made to be
our safe inventory of pain. And I was wrong.

The Emigrant Irish

Like oil lamps we put them out the back,

of our houses, of our minds. We had lights
better than, newer than and then

a time came, this time and now
we need them. Their dread, makeshift example.

They would have thrived on our necessities.
What they survived we could not even live.
By their lights now it is time to
imagine how they stood there, what they stood with,
that their possessions may become our power.

Cardboard. Iron. Their hardships parcelled in them.
Patience. Fortitude. Long-suffering
in the bruise-coloured dusk of the New World.

And all the old songs. And nothing to lose.

The Glass King

*Isabella of Bavaria married Charles VI of France in 1385. In later years
his madness took the form of believing he was made from glass.*

When he is ready he is raised and carried
among his vaporish plants; the palms and ferns flex;
they almost bend; you'd almost think they were going to kiss him;
and so they might; but she will not, his wife,

no she can't kiss his lips in case he splinters
into a million Bourbons, mad pieces.
What can she do with him – her daft prince?
His nightmares are the Regency of France.

Yes, she's been through it all, his Bavaroise,
blub-hipped and docile, urgent to be needed –
from churching to milk fever, from tongue-tied princess
to the queen of a mulish king – and now this.

They were each other's fantasy in youth.
No splintering at all about that mouth
when they were flesh and muscle, woman and man,
fire and kindling. See that silk divan?

Enough said. Now the times themselves
are his asylum: these are the Middle Ages, sweet
and savage era of the saving grace; indulgences
are two a penny; under the stonesmith's hand

stone turns into lace. I need his hand now.
Outside my window October soaks the stone;
you can hear it; you'd almost think
the brick was drinking it; the rowan drips

and history waits. Let it wait. I want
no elsewheres: the clover-smelling, stove-warm
air of autumn catches cold; the year turns;
the leaves fall; the poem hesitates:

If we could see ourselves, not as we do –
in mirrors, self-deceptions, self-regardings –
but as we ought to be and as we have been:
poets, lute-stringers, makyres and abettors

of our necessary art, soothsayers of the ailment
and disease of our times, sweet singers,
truth tellers, intercessors for self-knowledge –
what would we think of these fin-de-siècle

half-hearted penitents we have become
at the sick-bed of the century: hand-wringing
elegists with an ill-concealed greed
for the inheritance?
                                        My prince, demented

in a crystal past, a lost France, I elect you emblem
and ancestor of our lyric: it fits you like a glove –
doesn't it? – the part; untouchable, outlandish,
esoteric, inarticulate and out of reach

of human love: studied every day by your wife,
an ordinary honest woman out of place
in all this, wanting nothing more than the man
she married, all her sorrows in her stolid face.

from OUTSIDE HISTORY

1990

I Object Lessons

The Black Lace Fan My Mother Gave Me

It was the first gift he ever gave her,
buying it for five francs in the Galeries
in pre-war Paris. It was stifling.
A starless drought made the nights stormy.

They stayed in the city for the summer.
They met in cafés. She was always early.
He was late. That evening he was later.
They wrapped the fan. He looked at his watch.

She looked down the Boulevard des Capucines.
She ordered more coffee. She stood up.
The streets were emptying. The heat was killing.
She thought the distance smelled of rain and lightning.

These are wild roses, appliqued on silk by hand,
darkly picked, stitched boldly, quickly.
The rest is tortoiseshell and has the reticent,
clear patience of its element. It is

a worn-out, underwater bullion and it keeps,
even now, an inference of its violation.
The lace is overcast as if the weather
it opened for and offset had entered it.

The past is an empty café terrace.
An airless dusk before thunder. A man running.
And no way now to know what happened then –
none at all – unless, of course, you improvise:

The blackbird on this first sultry morning,
in summer, finding buds, worms, fruit,
feels the heat. Suddenly she puts out her wing –
the whole, full flirtatious span of it.

The Rooms of Other Women Poets

I wonder about you: whether the blue abrasions
of daylight, falling as dusk across your page,

make you reach for the lamp. I sometimes think
I see that gesture in the way you use language.

And whether you think, as I do, that wild flowers
dried and fired on the ironstone rim of

the saucer underneath your cup, are a sign of
a savage, old calligraphy: you will not have it.

The chair you use, for instance, may be cane
soaked and curled in spirals, painted white

and eloquent, or iron mesh and the table
a horizon of its own on plain, deal trestles,

bearing up unmarked, steel–cut foolscap,
a whole quire of it; when you leave I know

you look at them and you love their air of
unaggressive silence as you close the door.

The early summer, its covenant, its grace,
is everywhere: even shadows have leaves.

Somewhere you are writing or have written in
a room you came to as I come to this

room with honeyed corners, the interior sunless,
the windows shut but clear so I can see

the bay windbreak, the laburnum hang fire, feel
the ache of things ending in the jasmine darkening early.

The Shadow Doll

*This was sent to the bride-to-be in Victorian times, by her dressmaker.
It consisted in a porcelain doll, under a dome of glass, modelling
the proposed wedding dress.*

They stitched blooms from ivory tulle
to hem the oyster gleam of the veil.
They made hoops for the crinoline.

Now, in summary and neatly sewn –
a porcelain bride in an airless glamour –
the shadow doll survives its occasion.

Under glass, under wraps, it stays
even now, after all, discreet about
visits, fevers, quickenings and lusts

and just how, when she looked at
the shell-tone spray of seed pearls,
the bisque features, she could see herself

inside it all, holding less than real
stephanotis, rose petals, never feeling
satin rise and fall with the vows

I kept repeating on the night before –
astray among the cards and wedding gifts –
the coffee pots and the clocks and

the battered tan case full of cotton
lace and tissue-paper, pressing down, then
pressing down again. And then, locks.

The Latin Lesson

Easter light in the convent garden.
The eucalyptus tree glitters in it.
A bell rings for
the first class.

Today the Sixth Book of the *Aeneid*.
An old nun calls down the corridor.
Manners, girls. Where
are your manners?

Last night in his Lenten talk
the local priest asked us to remember
everything is put here
for a purpose:

even eucalyptus leaves are suitable
for making oil from to steep wool in,
to sweeten our blankets
and gaberdines.

My forefinger crawls on the lines.
A storm light comes in from the bay.
How beautiful the words
look, how

vagrant and strange on the page
before we crush them for their fragrance
        and crush them again
        to discover

the pathway to hell and that these
shadows in their shadow-bodies,
        chittering and mobbing
        on the far

shore, signalling their hunger for
the small usefulness of a life, are
        the dead. And how
        before the bell

will I hail the black keel and flatter the dark
boatman and cross the river and still
        keep a civil tongue
        in my head?

Bright-Cut Irish Silver

I take it down
from time to time, to feel
the smooth path of silver meet the cicatrice of skill.

These scars, I tell myself, are learned.

This gift for wounding an artery of rock
was passed on from father to son, to the father
of the next son;

is an aptitude
for injuring earth while inferring it in curves and surfaces;

is this cold potency which has come,
by time and chance,

into my hands.

II Outside History
A sequence

I The Achill Woman

She came up the hill carrying water.
She wore a half-buttoned, wool cardigan,
a tea-towel round her waist.

She pushed the hair out of her eyes with
her free hand and put the bucket down.

The zinc-music of the handle on the rim
tuned the evening. An Easter moon rose.
In the next-door field a stream was
a fluid sunset; and then, stars.

I remember the cold rosiness of her hands.
She bent down and blew on them like broth.
And round her waist, on a white background,
in coarse, woven letters, the words 'glass cloth'.

And she was nearly finished for the day.
And I was all talk, raw from college –
week-ending at a friend's cottage
with one suitcase and the set text
of the Court poets of the Silver Age.

We stayed putting down time until
the evening turned cold without warning.
She said goodnight and started down the hill.

The grass changed from lavender to black.
The trees turned back to cold outlines.
You could taste frost

but nothing now can change the way I went
indoors, chilled by the wind
and made a fire
and took down my book
and opened it and failed to comprehend

the harmonies of servitude,
the grace music gives to flattery
and language borrows from ambition –

and how I fell asleep
oblivious to

the planets clouding over in the skies,
the slow decline of the spring moon,
the songs crying out their ironies.

II   A False Spring

Alders are tasselled.
Flag-iris is already out on the canal.

From my window I can see
the College gardens, crocuses stammering
in pools of rain, plum blossom
on the branches.

I want to find her,
the woman I once was,
who came out of that reading-room

in a hard January, after studying
Aeneas in the underworld,

how his old battle-foes spotted him there –

how they called and called and called
only to have it be
a yell of shadows, an O vanishing in
the polished waters
and the topsy-turvy seasons of hell –

her mind so frail her body was its ghost.

I want to tell her she can rest,
she is embodied now.

But narcissi,
opening too early,
are all I find.
I hear the bad sound of these south winds,
the rain coming from some region which has lost sight
of our futures, leaving us
nothing to look forward to except
what one serious frost can accomplish.

III   The Making of an Irish Goddess

Ceres went to hell
with no sense of time.

When she looked back
all that she could see was

the arteries of silver in the rock,
the diligence of rivers always at one level,
wheat at one height,
leaves of a single colour,
the same distance in the usual light;

a seasonless, unscarred earth.

But I need time –
my flesh and that history –
to make the same descent.

In my body,
neither young now nor fertile,
and with the marks of childbirth
still on it,

in my gestures –
the way I pin my hair to hide
the stitched, healed blemish of a scar –
must be

an accurate inscription
of that agony:

the failed harvests,
the fields rotting to the horizon,
the children devoured by their mothers
whose souls, they would have said,
went straight to hell,
followed by their own.

There is no other way:

myth is the wound we leave
in the time we have

which in my case is this
March evening
at the foothills of the Dublin mountains,
across which the lights have changed all day,

holding up my hand,
sickle-shaped, to my eyes
to pick out
my own daughter from
all the other children in the distance;

her back turned to me.

IV   White Hawthorn in the West of Ireland

I drove West
in the season between seasons.
I left behind suburban gardens.
Lawnmowers. Small talk.

Under low skies, past splashes of coltsfoot,
I assumed
the hard shyness of Atlantic light
and the superstitious aura of hawthorn.

All I wanted then was to fill my arms with
sharp flowers,
to seem, from a distance, to be part of
that ivory, downhill rush. But I knew,

I had always known
the custom was
not to touch hawthorn.
Not to bring it indoors for the sake of

the luck
such constraint would forfeit –
a child might die, perhaps, or an unexplained
fever speckle heifers. So I left it

stirring on those hills
with a fluency
only water has. And, like water, able
to re-define land. And free to seem to be –

for anglers,
and for travellers astray in
the unmarked lights of a May dusk –
the only language spoken in those parts.

V Daphne Heard with Horror the Addresses of the God

It was early summer. Already
the conservatory was all steam and greenness.
I would have known the stephanotis by
its cut-throat sweetness anywhere.
We drank tea. You were telling me
a story you had heard as a child,
about the wedding of a local girl,
long ago, and a merchant from Argyll.

I thought the garden looked so at ease.
The roses were beginning on one side.
The laurel hedge was nothing but itself,
and all of it so free of any need
for nymphs, goddesses, wounded presences –
the fleet river-daughters who took root
and can be seen in the woods in
unmistakable shapes of weeping.

You were still speaking. By the time
I paid attention they were well married:
the bridegroom had his bride on the ship.
The sails were ready to be set. You said
small craft went with her to the ship and,
as it sailed out, well-wishers
took in armfuls, handfuls, from the boats
white roses and threw them on the water.

We cleared up then, saying how
the greenfly needed spraying, the azaleas
were over; and you went inside. I
stayed in the heat looking out at
the garden in its last definition.
Freshening and stirring. A suggestion,
behind it all, of darkness. In the shadow,
beside the laurel hedge, its gesture.

VI *The Photograph on My Father's Desk*

It could be
any summer afternoon.

The sun is warm on
the fruitwood garden seat.
Fuchsia droops.
Thrushes move to get
windfalls underneath the crab apple tree.

The woman
holds her throat like a wound.

She wears
mutton-coloured gaberdine with
a scum of lace
just above her boot

which is pointed at
this man coming down the path with
his arms wide open. Laughing.

The garden fills up
with a burned silence.

The talk has stopped.
The spoon which just now
jingled at the rim of the lemonade jug

is still.
And the shrubbed lavender
will find
neither fragrance nor muslin.

VII   We Are Human History. We Are Not Natural History.

At twilight in
the shadow of the poplars
the children found a swarm of wild bees.

It was late summer and I knew as
they came shouting in that, yes,
this evening had been singled out by

a finger pointing at trees,
the inland feel of that greenness,
the sugar-barley iron of a garden chair

and children still bramble-height
and fretful from the heat and a final
brightness stickle-backing that particular

patch of grass across which light
was short-lived and elegiac as
the view from a train window of

a station parting, all tears. And this,
this I thought, is how it will have been
chosen from those summer evenings

which under the leaves of the poplars –
striped dun and ochre, simmering over
the stashed-up debris of old seasons –

a swarm of wild bees is making use of.

VIII   *An Old Steel Engraving*

Look.
The figure in the foreground breaks his fall with
one hand. He cannot die.
The river cannot wander
into the shadows to be dragged by willows.
The passer-by is scared witless. He cannot escape.
He cannot stop staring at
this hand which can barely raise
the patriot
above the ground which is
the origin and reason for it all.

More closely now:
at the stillness of unfinished action in
afternoon heat, at the spaces on the page. They widen
to include us:
we have found

the country of our malediction where
nothing can move until we find the word,
nothing can stir until we say this is

what happened and is happening and history
is one of us who turns away
while the other is
turning the page.

Is this river which
moments ago must have flashed the morse
of a bayonet thrust. And is moving on.

IX   In Exile

The German girls who came to us that winter and
the winter after and who helped my mother fuel
the iron stove and arranged our clothes in wet
thicknesses on the wooden rail after tea was over,

spoke no English, understood no French. They were
sisters from a ruined city and they spoke rapidly
in their own tongue: syllables in which pain was
radical, integral; and with what sense of injury

the language angled for an unhurt kingdom – for
the rise, curve, kill and swift return to the wrist,
to the hood – I never knew. To me they were the sounds
of evening only, of the cold, of the Irish dark and

continuous with all such recurrences: the drizzle in
the lilac, the dusk always at the back door, like
the tinkers I was threatened with, the cat inching
closer to the fire with its screen of clothes, where

I am standing in the stone-flagged kitchen; there are
bleached rags, perhaps, and a pot of tea on the stove.
And I see myself, four years of age and looking up,
storing such music – guttural, hurt to the quick –

as I hear now, forty years on and far from where
I heard it first. Among these salt-boxes, marshes and
the glove-tanned colours of the sugar-maples, in
this New England town at the start of winter, I am

so much south of it: the soft wet, the light and
those early darks which strengthen the assassin's
hand; and hide the wound. Here, in this scalding air,
my speech will not heal. I do not want it to heal.

X   We Are Always Too Late

Memory
is in two parts.

First, the re-visiting:

the way even now I can see
those lovers at the café table. She is weeping.

It is New England, breakfast-time, winter. Behind her,
outside the picture window, is
a stand of white pines.

New snow falls and the old,
losing its balance in the branches,
showers down,
adding fractions to it. Then

the re-enactment. Always that.
I am getting up, pushing away
coffee. Always, I am going towards her.

The flush and scald is
to her forehead now and back down to her neck.

I raise one hand. I am pointing to
those trees, I am showing her our need for these
beautiful upstagings of
what we suffer by
what survives. And she never even sees me.

XI   *What We Lost*

It is a winter afternoon.
The hills are frozen. Light is failing.
The distance is a crystal earshot.
A woman is mending linen in her kitchen.

She is a countrywoman.
Behind her cupboard doors she hangs sprigged,
stove-dried lavender in muslin.
Her letters and mementoes and memories

are packeted in satin at the back with
gaberdine and worsted and
the cambric she has made into bodices;
the good tobacco silk for Sunday Mass.

She is sewing in the kitchen.
The sugar-feel of flax is in her hands.
Dusk. And the candles brought in then.
One by one. And the quiet sweat of wax.

There is a child at her side.
The tea is poured, the stitching put down.
The child grows still, sensing something of importance.
The woman settles and begins her story.

Believe it, what we lost is here in this room
on this veiled evening.
The woman finishes. The story ends.
The child, who is my mother, gets up, moves away.

In the winter air, unheard, unshared,
the moment happens, hangs fire, leads nowhere.
The light will fail and the room darken,
the child fall asleep and the story be forgotten.

The fields are dark already.
The frail connections have been made and are broken.
The dumb-show of legend has become language,
is becoming silence and who will know that once

words were possibilities and disappointments,
were scented closets filled with love-letters
and memories and lavender hemmed into muslin,
stored in sachets, aired in bed-linen;

and travelled silks and the tones of cotton
tautened into bodices, subtly shaped by breathing;
were the rooms of childhood with their griefless peace,
their hands and whispers, their candles weeping brightly?

XII   Outside History

There are outsiders, always. These stars –
these iron inklings of an Irish January,
whose light happened

thousands of years before
our pain did: they are, they have always been
outside history.

They keep their distance. Under them remains
a place where you found
you were human and

a landscape in which you know you are mortal.
And a time to choose between them.
I have chosen:

out of myth into history I move to be
part of that ordeal
whose darkness is

only now reaching me from those fields,
those rivers, those roads clotted as
firmaments with the dead.

How slowly they die
as we kneel beside them, whisper in their ear.
And we are too late. We are always too late.

III Distances

Distances

The radio is playing downstairs in the kitchen.
The clock says eight and the light says
winter. You are pulling up your hood against a bad morning.

Don't leave, I say. Don't go without telling me
the name of that song. You call it back to me from the stairs –
'I Wish I Was In Carrickfergus'

and the words open out with emigrant grief the way the streets
of a small town open out in
memory: salt-loving fuchsias to one side and

a market in full swing on the other with
linen for sale and tacky apples and a glass and wire hill
of spectacles on a metal tray. The front door bangs

and you're gone. I will think of it all morning while a fine
drizzle closes in, making the distances
fiction: not of that place but this and of how

restless we would be, you and I, inside the perfect
music of that basalt and sandstone
coastal town. We would walk the streets in

the scentless afternoon of a ballad measure,
longing to be able
to tell each other that the starched lace and linen of

adult handkerchiefs scraped your face and left your tears
falling; how the apples were mush inside the crisp sugar
shell and the spectacles out of focus.

Midnight Flowers

I go down step by step.
The house is quiet, full of trapped heat and sleep.
In the kitchen everything is still.
Nothing is distinct; there is no moon to speak of.

I could be undone every single day by
paradox or what they call in the countryside
blackthorn winter,
when hailstones come with the first apple blossom.

I turn a switch and the garden grows.
A whole summer's work in one instant!
I press my face to the glass. I can see
shadows of lilac, of fuchsia; a dark likeness of blackcurrant:

little clients of suddenness, how sullen they are at
the margins of the light.
They need no rain, they have no roots.
I reach out a hand; they are gone.

When I was a child a snapdragon was
held an inch from my face. Look, a voice said, this
is the colour of your hair. And there it was, my head,
a pliant jewel in the hands of someone else.

Our Origins Are in the Sea

I live near the coast. On these summer nights
the dog-star rises somewhere near the hunter,
near the sun. I stand at the edge of our grass.

I do not connect them: once they were connected –
the fixity of stars and unruly salt water –
by sailors with an avarice for landfall.

And this is land. The way the whitebeams will
begin their fall to an alluvial earth and
a bicycle wheel is spinning on it, proves that.

From where I stand the sea is just a rumour.
The stars are put out by our streetlamp. Light
and seawater are well separated. And how little

survives of the sea-captain in his granddaughter
is everywhere apparent. Such things get lost.
He drowned in the Bay of Biscay. I never saw him.

I turn to go in. The hills are indistinct.
The coast is near and darkening. The stars are clearer.
The grass and the house are lapped in shadow.

And the briar rose is rigged in the twilight,
the way I imagine sails used to be –
lacy and stiff together, a frigate of ivory.

What Love Intended

I can imagine if,
I came back again,
 looking through windows at

broken mirrors, pictures,
and, in the cracked upstairs,
 the beds where it all began.

The suburb in the rain
this October morning,
 full of food and children

and animals, will be –
when I come back again –
 gone to rack and ruin.

I will be its ghost,
its revenant, discovering
 again in one place

the history of my pain,
my ordeal, my grace,
 unable to resist

seeing what is past,
judging what has ended
 and whether, first to last,

from then to now and even
here, ruined, this
 is what love intended –

finding even the yellow
jasmine in the dusk,
 the smell of early dinners,

the voices of our children,
taking turns and quarrelling,
    burned on the distance,

    gone. And the small square
where under cropped lime
    and poplar, on bicycles

    and skates in the summer,
they played until dark;
    propitiating time.

    And even the two whitebeams
outside the house gone, with
    the next-door-neighbour

    who used to say in April –
when one was slow to bloom –
    they were a man and woman.

from IN A TIME OF VIOLENCE

1994

The Singers

for M.R.

The women who were singers in the West
lived on an unforgiving coast.
I want to ask was there ever one
moment when all of it relented,
when rain and ocean and their own
sense of home were revealed to them
as one and the same?
                          After which
every day was still shaped by weather,
but every night their mouths filled with
Atlantic storms and clouded-over stars
and exhausted birds.
                          And only when the danger
was plain in the music could you know
their true measure of rejoicing in

finding a voice where they found a vision.

I Writing in a Time of Violence
A sequence

*As in a city where the evil are permitted to have authority and the good
are put out of the way, so in the soul of man, as we maintain,
the imitative poet implants an evil constitution, for he indulges the
irrational nature which has no discernment of greater or less.*

Plato, *The Republic*, X

1 *That the Science of Cartography is Limited*

– and not simply by the fact that this shading of
forest cannot show the fragrance of balsam,
the gloom of cypresses
is what I wish to prove.

When you and I were first in love we drove
to the borders of Connacht
and entered a wood there.

Look down you said: this was once a famine road.

I looked down at ivy and the scutch grass
rough–cast stone had
disappeared into as you told me
in the second winter of their ordeal, in

1847, when the crop had failed twice,
Relief Committees gave
the starving Irish such roads to build.

Where they died, there the road ended

and ends still and when I take down
the map of this island, it is never so
I can say here is
the masterful, the apt rendering of

the spherical as flat, nor
an ingenious design which persuades a curve
into a plane,
but to tell myself again that

the line which says woodland and cries hunger
and gives out among sweet pine and cypress
and finds no horizon

will not be there.

2   *The Death of Reason*

When the Peep-O-Day Boys were laying fires down in
the hayricks and seed-barns of a darkening Ireland,
the art of portrait-painting reached its height
across the water.
The fire caught.
The flames cracked and the light showed up the scaffold
and the wind carried staves of a ballad.
The flesh-smell of hatred.
And she climbed the stairs.
Nameless composite. Anonymous beauty-bait for the painter.
Rustling gun-coloured silks. To set a seal on Augustan London.
And sat down.
The easel waits for her
and the age is ready to resemble her and
the small breeze cannot touch that powdered hair.
That elegance.
But I smell fire.

From Antrim to the Boyne the sky is reddening as
the painter tints alizerine crimson with a mite of yellow
mixed once with white and finds out
how difficult it is to make the skin
blush outside the skin.
The flames have crossed the sea.
They are at the lintel. At the door.
At the canvas,
at her mouth.
And the curve and pout
of supple dancing and the couplet rhyming
and the pomander scenting death-rooms and
the cabinet-maker setting his veneers
in honest wood – they are kindling for the flames.
And the dictates of reason and the blended sensibility
of tact and proportion – yes
the eighteenth century ends here
as her hem scorches and the satin
decoration catches fire. She is burning down.
As a house might. As a candle will.
She is ash and tallow. It is over.

3   March 1 1847. By the First Post

The daffodils are out & how
you would love the harebells by
the Blackwater now.
But Etty, you are wise to stay away.
London may be dull in this season.
Meath is no better I assure you.
Your copper silk is sewn
& will be sent & I envy you.
No one talks of anything but famine.
I go nowhere –

not from door to carriage – but a cloth
sprinkled with bay rum & rose attar
is pressed against my mouth.
Our picnics by the river –
remember that one with Major Harris? –
our outings to the opera
& our teas
are over now for the time being.
Shall I tell you what I saw on Friday,
driving with Mama? A woman lying
across the Kells Road with her baby –
in full view. We had to go
out of our way
to get home & we were late
& poor Mama was not herself all day.

4   In a Bad Light

This is St Louis. Where the rivers meet.
    The Illinois. The Mississippi. The Missouri.
The light is in its element of autumn.
    Clear. With yellow gingko leaves falling.
There is always a nightmare. Even in such light.

The weather must be cold now in Dublin.
    And when skies are clear frosts come
down on the mountains and the first
    inklings of winter will be underfoot in
the crisp iron of a fern at dawn.

I stand in a room in the Museum.
    In one glass case a plastic figure
represents a woman in a dress,
    with crêpe sleeves and a satin apron.
And feet laced neatly into suede.

She stands in a replica of a cabin
　　　on a steamboat bound for New Orleans.
The year is 1860. Nearly war.
　　　　A notice says no comforts were spared. The silk
is French. The seamstresses are Irish.

I see them in the oil-lit parlours.
　　　I am in the gas-lit backrooms.
We make in the apron front and from
　　　the papery appearance and crushable
look of crêpe, a sign. We are bent over

in a bad light. We are sewing a last
　　　sight of shore. We are sewing coffin ships.
And the salt of exile. And our own
　　　death in it. For history's abandonment
we are doing this. And this. And

this is a button hole. This is a stitch.
　　　Fury enters them the way frost follows
every arabesque and curl of a fern: this is
　　　the nightmare. See how you perceive it.
We sleep the sleep of exhaustion.

We dream a woman on a steamboat
　　　parading in sunshine in a dress we know
we made. She laughs off rumours of war.
　　　She turns and traps light on the skirt.
It is, for that moment, beautiful.

5   The Dolls Museum in Dublin

The wounds are terrible. The paint is old.
The cracks along the lips and on the cheeks
cannot be fixed. The cotton lawn is soiled.
The arms are ivory dissolved to wax.

Recall the quadrille. Hum the waltz.
Promenade on the yacht-club terraces.
Put back the lamps in their copper holders,
the carriage wheels on the cobbled quays.

And recreate Easter in Dublin.
Booted officers. Their mistresses.
Sunlight criss-crossing College Green.
Steam hissing from the flanks of horses.

Here they are. Cradled and cleaned,
held close in the arms of their owners.
Their cold hands clasped by warm hands,
their faces memorised like perfect manners.

The altars are mannerly with linen.
The lilies are whiter than surplices.
The candles are burning and warning:
Rejoice, they whisper. After sacrifice.

Horse chestnuts hold up their candles.
The Green is vivid with parasols.
Sunlight is pastel and windless.
The bar of the Shelbourne is full.

Laughter and gossip on the terraces.
Rumour and alarm at the barracks.
The Empire is summoning its officers.
The carriages are turning: they are turning back.

Past children walking with governesses,
Looking down, cossetting their dolls,
then looking up as the carriage passes,
the shadow chilling them. Twilight falls.

It is twilight in the dolls museum. Shadows
remain on the parchment-coloured waists,
are bruises on the stitched cotton clothes,
are hidden in the dimples on the wrists.

The eyes are wide. They cannot address
the helplessness which has lingered in
the airless peace of each glass case:
to have survived. To have been stronger than

a moment. To be the hostages ignorance
takes from time and ornament from destiny. Both.
To be the present of the past. To infer the difference
with a terrible stare. But not feel it. And not know it.

6   Inscriptions

About holiday rooms there can be
a solid feel at first. Then, as you go upstairs,
the air gets
a dry rustle of excitement

the way a new dress comes out of tissue paper,
up and out of it, and
the girl watching this thinks:
Where will I wear it? Who will kiss me in it?

Peter
was the name on the cot.
The cot was made of the carefully bought
scarcities of the nineteen-forties:
oak. Tersely planed and varnished.
Cast-steel hinges.

I stood where the roof sloped into
paper roses,
in a room where a child once went to sleep,
looking at blue, painted lettering:

as he slept
someone had found for him
five pieces of the alphabet which said
the mauve petals of his eyelids as they closed out
the scalded hallway moonlight made of the ocean at
the end of his road.

Someone knew
the importance of giving him a name.

For years I have known
how important it is
not to name
the coffins, the murdered in them,
the deaths in alleyways and on doorsteps –

in case they rise out of their names
and I recognise

the child who slept peacefully
and the girl who guessed at her future in
the dress as it came out of its box
falling free in
kick pleats of silk.

And what comfort can there be
in knowing that
in a distant room
his sign is safe tonight
and reposes its modest blues in darkness?

Or that outside his window
the name-eating elements – the salt wind, the rain –
must find
headstones to feed their hunger?

7 Beautiful Speech

In my last year in College
I set out
to write an essay on
the Art of Rhetoric. I had yet to find

the country already lost to me
in song and figure as I scribbled down
names for sweet euphony
and safe digression.

And when I came to the word *insinuate*
I saw that language could writhe and creep
and the lore of snakes
which I had learned as a child not to fear –
because the Saint had sent them out of Ireland –
came nearer.

Chiasmus. Litotes. Periphrasis. Old
indices and agents of persuasion. How
I remember them in that room where
a girl is writing at a desk with
dusk already in
the streets outside. I can see her. I could say to her –

we will live, we have lived
where language is concealed. Is perilous.
We will be – we have been – citizens
of its hiding place. But it is too late

to shut the book of satin phrases,
to refuse to enter
an evening bitter with peat smoke,
where newspaper sellers shout headlines
and friends call out their farewells in
a city of whispers
and interiors where

the dear vowels
Irish Ireland ours are
absorbed into autumn air,
are out of earshot in the distances
we are stepping into where we never

imagine words such as *hate*
and *territory* and the like – unbanished still
as they always would be – wait
and are waiting under
beautiful speech. To strike.

II Legends

This Moment

A neighbourhood.
At dusk.

Things are getting ready
to happen
out of sight.

Stars and moths.
And rinds slanting around fruit.

But not yet.

One tree is black.
One window is yellow as butter.

A woman leans down to catch a child
who has run into her arms
this moment.

Stars rise.
Moths flutter.
Apples sweeten in the dark.

Love

Dark falls on this mid-western town
where we once lived when myths collided.
Dusk has hidden the bridge in the river
which slides and deepens
to become the water
the hero crossed on his way to hell.

Not far from here is our old apartment.
We had a kitchen and an Amish table.
We had a view. And we discovered there
love had the feather and muscle of wings
and had come to live with us,
a brother of fire and air.

We had two infant children one of whom
was touched by death in this town
and spared: and when the hero
was hailed by his comrades in hell
their mouths opened and their voices failed and
there is no knowing what they would have asked
about a life they had shared and lost.

I am your wife.
It was years ago.
Our child is healed. We love each other still.
Across our day-to-day and ordinary distances
we speak plainly. We hear each other clearly.

And yet I want to return to you
on the bridge of the Iowa river as you were,
with snow on the shoulders of your coat
and a car passing with its headlights on:

I see you as a hero in a text –
the image blazing and the edges gilded –
and I long to cry out the epic question
my dear companion:

Will we ever live so intensely again?
Will love come to us again and be
so formidable at rest it offered us ascension
even to look at him?

But the words are shadows and you cannot hear me.
You walk away and I cannot follow.

The Pomegranate

The only legend I have ever loved is
the story of a daughter lost in hell.
And found and rescued there.
Love and blackmail are the gist of it.
Ceres and Persephone the names.
And the best thing about the legend is
I can enter it anywhere. And have.
As a child in exile in
a city of fogs and strange consonants,
I read it first and at first I was
an exiled child in the crackling dusk of
the underworld, the stars blighted. Later
I walked out in a summer twilight
searching for my daughter at bed-time.
When she came running I was ready
to make any bargain to keep her.
I carried her back past whitebeams
and wasps and honey-scented buddleias.
But I was Ceres then and I knew

winter was in store for every leaf
on every tree on that road.
Was inescapable for each one we passed.
And for me.
                    It is winter
and the stars are hidden.
I climb the stairs and stand where I can see
my child asleep beside her teen magazines,
her can of Coke, her plate of uncut fruit.
The pomegranate! How did I forget it?
She could have come home and been safe
and ended the story and all
our heart-broken searching but she reached
out a hand and plucked a pomegranate.
She put out her hand and pulled down
the French sound for apple and
the noise of stone and the proof
that even in the place of death,
at the heart of legend, in the midst
of rocks full of unshed tears
ready to be diamonds by the time
the story was told, a child can be
hungry. I could warn her. There is still a chance.
The rain is cold. The road is flint-coloured.
The suburb has cars and cable television.
The veiled stars are above ground.
It is another world. But what else
can a mother give her daughter but such
beautiful rifts in time?
If I defer the grief I will diminish the gift.
The legend will be hers as well as mine.
She will enter it. As I have.
She will wake up. She will hold
the papery flushed skin in her hand.
And to her lips. I will say nothing.

Moths

Tonight the air smells of cut grass.
Apples rust on the branches. Already summer is
a place mislaid between expectation and memory.

This has been a summer of moths.
Their moment of truth comes well after dark.
Then they reveal themselves at our windowledges
and sills as a pinpoint. A glimmer.

The books I look up about them are full of legends:
ghost-swift moths with their dancing assemblies at dusk.
Their courtship swarms. How some kinds may steer by the moon.

The moon is up. The back windows are wide open.
Mid-July light fills the neighbourhood. I stand by the hedge.

Once again they are near the windowsill –
fluttering past the fuchsia and the lavender,
which is knee-high, and too blue to warn them

they will fall down without knowing how
or why what they steered by became, suddenly,
what they crackled and burned around. They will perish –

I am perishing – on the edge and at the threshold of
the moment all nature fears and tends towards:

the stealing of the light. Ingenious facsimile.

And the kitchen bulb which beckons them makes
my child's shadow longer than my own.

In Which the Ancient History I Learn Is Not My Own

The linen map
hung from the wall.
The linen was shiny
and cracked in places.
The cracks were darkened by grime.
It was fastened to the classroom wall with
a wooden batten on
a triangle of knotted cotton.

The colours
were faded out
so the red of Empire –
the stain of absolute possession –
the mark once made from Kashmir
to the oast-barns of the Kent
coast south of us was
underwater coral.

Ireland was far away
and farther away
every year.
I was nearly an English child.
I could list the English kings.
I could name the famous battles.
I was learning to recognise
God's grace in history.

And the waters
of the Irish sea,
their shallow weave
and cross-grained blue green
had drained away
to the pale gaze
of a doll's china eyes –
a stare without recognition or memory.

We have no oracles,
no rocks or olive trees,
no sacred path to the temple
and no priestesses.
The teacher's voice had a London accent.
This was London. 1952.
It was Ancient History Class.
She put the tip

of the wooden
pointer on the map.
She tapped over ridges and dried-
out rivers and cities buried in
the sea and sea-scapes which
had once been land.
And stopped.
Remember this, children.

The Roman Empire was
the greatest Empire
ever known —
until our time of course —
while the Delphic Oracle
was reckoned to be
the exact centre
of the earth.

Suddenly
I wanted
to stand in front of it.
I wanted to trace over
and over the weave of my own country.
To read out names
I was close to forgetting.
Wicklow. Kilruddery. Dublin.

To ask
where exactly
was my old house?
Its brass One and Seven.
Its flight of granite steps.
Its lilac tree whose scent
stayed under your fingernails
for days.

For days –
she was saying – *even months,*
the ancients travelled
to the Oracle.
They brought sheep and killed them.
They brought questions about tillage and war.
They rarely left with more
than an ambiguous answer.

The Parcel

There are dying arts and
one of them is
the way my mother used to make up a parcel.
Paper first. Mid-brown and coarse-grained as wood.
The worst sort for covering a Latin book neatly
or laying flat at Christmas on a pudding bowl.
It was a big cylinder. She snipped it open
and it unrolled quickly across the floor.
All business, all distance.
Then the scissors.
Not a glittering let-up but a dour
pair, black thumb-holes,
the shears themselves the colour of the rained-
on steps a man with a grindstone climbed up

in the season of lilac and snapdragon
and stood there arguing the rate for
sharpening the lawnmower and the garden pair
and this one. All-in.
The ball of twine was coarsely braided
and only a shade less yellow than
the flame she held under the blunt
end of the sealing-wax until
it melted and spread into a brittle
terracotta medal.
Her hair dishevelled, her tongue between her teeth,
she wrote the address in the quarters
twine had divided the surface into.
Names and places. Crayon and fountain-pen.
The town underlined once. The country twice.
It's ready for the post
she would say and if we want to know
where it went to –
a craft lost before we missed it – watch it go
into the burlap sack for collection.
See it disappear. Say
this is how it died
out: among doomed steamships and out-dated trains,
the tracks for them disappearing before our eyes,
next to station names we can't remember
on a continent we no longer
recognise. The sealing-wax cracking.
The twine unravelling. The destination illegible.

Lava Cameo

a brooch carved on volcanic rock

I like this story –

My grandfather was a sea-captain.
My grandmother always met him when his ship docked.
She feared the women at the ports –

except that it is not a story,
more a rumour or a folk memory,
something thrown out once in a random conversation;
a hint merely.

If I say wool and lace for her skirt and
crêpe for her blouse
in the neck of which is pinned a cameo,
carved out of black, volcanic rock;

if I make her pace the Cork docks, stopping
to take down her parasol as a gust catches
the silk tassels of it –

then consider this:

there is a way of making free with the past,
a pastiche of what is
real and what is
not, which can only be
justified if you think of it

not as sculpture but syntax:
a structure extrinsic to meaning which uncovers
the inner secret of it.

She will die at thirty-one in a fever ward.
He will drown nine years later in the Bay of Biscay.
They will never even be
sepia and so I put down

the gangplank now between the ship and the ground.
In the story, late afternoon has become evening.
They kiss once, their hands touch briefly.
Please.

Look at me, I want to say to her: show me
the obduracy of an art which can
arrest a profile in the flux of hell.

Inscribe catastrophe.

Legends

for Eavan Frances

Tryers of firesides,
twilights. There are no tears in these.

Instead, they begin the world again,
making the mountain ridges blue
and the rivers clear and the hero fearless –

and the outcome always undecided
so the next teller can say *begin* and
again and astonish children.

Our children are our legends.
You are mine. You have my name.
My hair was once like yours.

And the world
is less bitter to me
because you will re-tell the story.

III Anna Liffey

Anna Liffey

Life, the story goes,
Was the daughter of Cannan,
And came to the plain of Kildare.
She loved the flat-lands and the ditches
And the unreachable horizon.
She asked that it be named for her.
The river took its name from the land.
The land took its name from a woman.

A woman in the doorway of a house.
A river in the city of her birth.

There, in the hills above my house,
The river Liffey rises, is a source.
It rises in rush and ling heather and
Black peat and bracken and strengthens
To claim the city it narrated.
Swans. Steep falls. Small towns.
The smudged air and bridges of Dublin.

Dusk is coming.
Rain is moving east from the hills.

If I could see myself
I would see
A woman in a doorway
Wearing the colours that go with red hair.
Although my hair is no longer red.

I praise
The gifts of the river.
Its shiftless and glittering
Re-telling of a city,
Its clarity as it flows,
In the company of runt flowers and herons,
Around a bend at Islandbridge
And under thirteen bridges to the sea.
Its patience at twilight –
Swans nesting by it,
Neon wincing into it.

Maker of
Places, remembrances,
Narrate such fragments for me:

One body. One spirit.
One place. One name.
The city where I was born.
The river that runs through it.
The nation which eludes me.

Fractions of a life
It has taken me a lifetime
To claim.

I came here in a cold winter.

I had no children. No country.
I did not know the name for my own life.

My country took hold of me.
My children were born.

I walked out in a summer dusk
To call them in.

One name. Then the other one.
The beautiful vowels sounding out home.

Make of a nation what you will
Make of the past
What you can –

There is now
A woman in a doorway.

It has taken me
All my strength to do this.

Becoming a figure in a poem.

Usurping a name and a theme.

A river is not a woman.
   Although the names it finds,
      The history it makes
And suffers –
   The Viking blades beside it,
      The muskets of the Redcoats,
         The flames of the Four Courts
Blazing into it
   Are a sign.
         Any more than
A woman is a river,
   Although the course it takes,
      Through swans courting and distraught willows,
Its patience
   Which is also its powerlessness,
      From Callary to Islandbridge,
         And from source to mouth,
Is another one.
               And in my late forties
Past believing
      Love will heal
         What language fails to know
And needs to say –
   What the body means –
         I take this sign
And I make this mark:
      A woman in the doorway of her house.
         A river in the city of her birth.
The truth of a suffered life.
         The mouth of it.

The seabirds come in from the coast.
The city wisdom is they bring rain.
I watch them from my doorway.
I see them as arguments of origin –
Leaving a harsh force on the horizon
Only to find it
Slanting and falling elsewhere.

Which water –
The one they leave or the one they pronounce –
Remembers the other?

I am sure
The body of an ageing woman
Is a memory
And to find a language for it
Is as hard
As weeping and requiring
These birds to cry out as if they could
Recognise their element
Remembered and diminished in
A single tear.

An ageing woman
Finds no shelter in language.
She finds instead
Single words she once loved
Such as 'summer' and 'yellow'
And 'sexual' and 'ready'
Have suddenly become dwellings
For someone else –
Rooms and a roof under which someone else
Is welcome, not her. Tell me,
Anna Liffey,
Spirit of water,
Spirit of place,
How is it on this
Rainy autumn night

As the Irish sea takes
The names you made, the names
You bestowed, and gives you back
Only wordlessness?

Autumn rain is
Scattering and dripping
From car-ports
And clipped hedges.
The gutters are full.

When I came here
I had neither
Children nor country.
The trees were arms.
The hills were dreams.

I was free
To imagine a spirit
In the blues and greens,
The hills and fogs
Of a small city.

My children were born.
My country took hold of me.
A vision in a brick house.
Is it only love
That makes a place?

I feel it change.
My children are
Growing up, getting older.
My country holds on
To its own pain.

I turn off
The harsh yellow
Porch light and
Stand in the hall.
Where is home now?

Follow the rain
Out to the Dublin hills.
Let it become the river.
Let the spirit of place be
A lost soul again.

In the end
It will not matter
That I was a woman. I am sure of it.
The body is a source. Nothing more.
There is a time for it. There is a certainty
About the way it seeks its own dissolution.
Consider rivers.
They are always en route to
Their own nothingness. From the first moment
They are going home. And so
When language cannot do it for us,
Cannot make us know love will not diminish us,
There are these phrases
Of the ocean
To console us.
Particular and unafraid of their completion.
In the end
Everything that burdened and distinguished me
Will be lost in this:
I was a voice.

Time and Violence

The evening was the same as any other.
I came out and stood on the step.
The suburb was closed in the weather

of an early spring and the shallow tips
and washed-out yellows of narcissi
resisted dusk. And crocuses and snowdrops.

I stood there and felt the melancholy
of growing older in such a season,
when all I could be certain of was simply

in this time of fragrance and refrain,
whatever else might flower before the fruit,
and be renewed, I would not. Not again.

A car splashed by in the twilight.
Peat smoke stayed in the windless
air overhead and I might have missed it:

a presence. Suddenly. In the very place
where I would stand in other dusks, and look
to pick out my child from the distance,

was a shepherdess, her smile cracked,
her arm injured from the mantelpieces
and pastorals where she posed with her crook.

Then I turned and saw in the spaces
of the night sky constellations appear,
one by one, over roof-tops and houses,

and Cassiopeia trapped: stabbed where
her thigh met her groin and her hand
her glittering wrist, with the pin-point of a star.

And by the road where rain made standing
pools of water underneath cherry trees,
and blossoms swam on their images,

was a mermaid with invented tresses,
her breasts printed with the salt of it and all
the desolation of the North Sea in her face.

I went nearer. They were disappearing.
Dusk had turned to night but in the air –
did I imagine it? – a voice was saying:

*This is what language did to us. Here
is the wound, the silence, the wretchedness
of tides and hillsides and stars where*

*we languish in a grammar of sighs,
in the high-minded search for euphony,
in the midnight rhetoric of poesie.*

*We cannot sweat here. Our skin is icy.
We cannot breed here. Our wombs are empty.
Help us to escape youth and beauty.*

*Write us out of the poem. Make us human
in cadences of change and mortal pain
and words we can grow old and die in.*

A Woman Painted on a Leaf

I found it among curios and silver,
in the pureness of wintry light.

A woman painted on a leaf.

Fine lines drawn on a veined surface
in a hand-made frame.

This is not my face. Neither did I draw it.

A leaf falls in a garden.
The moon cools its aftermath of sap.
The pith of summer dries out in starlight.

A woman is inscribed there.

This is not death. It is the terrible
suspension of life.

I want a poem
I can grow old in. I want a poem I can die in.

I want to take
this dried-out face,
as you take a starling from behind iron,
and return it to its element of air, of ending –

so that autumn
which was once
the hard look of stars,
the frown on a gardener's face,
a gradual bronzing of the distance,

will be,
from now on,
a crisp tinder underfoot. Cheekbones. Eyes. Will be
a mouth crying out. Let me.

Let me die.

from THE LOST LAND

1998

I Colony

A sequence

1 My Country in Darkness

After the wolves and before the elms
the Bardic Order ended in Ireland.

Only a few remained to continue
a dead art in a dying land:

This is a man
on the road from Youghal to Cahirmoyle.
He has no comfort, no food and no future.
He has no fire to recite his friendless measures by.
His riddles and flatteries will have no reward.
His patrons sheath their swords in Flanders and Madrid.

Reader of poems, lover of poetry –
in case you thought this was a gentle art,
follow this man on a moonless night
to the wretched bed he will have to make:

The Gaelic world stretches out under a hawthorn tree
and burns in the rain. This is its home,
its last frail shelter. All of it –
Limerick, the Wild Geese and what went before –
falters into cadence before he sleeps:

He shuts his eyes. Darkness falls on it.

2 The Harbour

This harbour was made by art and force.
And called Kingstown and afterwards Dun Laoghaire.
And holds the sea behind its barrier
less than five miles from my house.

Lord be with us say the makers of a nation.
Lord look down say the builders of a harbour.
They came and cut a shape out of ocean
and left stone to close around their labour.

Officers and their wives promenaded
on this spot once and saw with their own eyes
the opulent horizon and obedient skies
which nine-tenths of the law provided.

And frigates with thirty-six guns cruising
the outer edges of influence could idle
and enter here and catch the tide of
empire and arrogance and the Irish sea rising

and rising through a century of storms
and cormorants and moonlight the whole length of this coast,
while an ocean forgot an empire and the armed
ships under it changed: to slime weed and cold salt and rust.

City of shadows and of the gradual
capitulations to the last invader
this is the final one: signed in water
and witnessed in granite and ugly bronze and gun-metal.

And by me. I am your citizen: composed of
your fictions, your compromise, I am
a part of your story and its outcome.
And ready to record its contradictions.

3 Witness

Here is the city –
its worn-down mountains,
its grass and iron,
its smoky coast
seen from the high roads
on the Wicklow side.

From Dalkey Island
to the North Wall,
to the blue distance seizing its perimeter,
its old divisions are deep within it.

And in me also.
And always will be:

Out of my mouth they come.
The spurred and booted garrisons.
The men and women
they dispossessed.

What is a colony
if not the brutal truth
that when we speak
the graves open.
And the dead walk?

4 Daughters of Colony

Daughters of parsons and of army men.
Daughters of younger sons of younger sons.
Who left for London from Kingstown harbour –
never certain which they belonged to.

Who took their journals and their steamer trunks.
Who took their sketching books.

Who wore hats
made out of local straw
dried in an Irish field beside a river which

flowed to a town they had known in childhood,
and watched forever from their bedroom windows,
framed in the clouds and cloud-shadows,
the blotchy cattle and

the scattered window lamps of a flat landscape
they could not enter.
Would never enter.

I see the darkness coming.
The absurd smallness of the handkerchiefs
they are waving
as the shore recedes.

I put my words between them
and the silence
the failing light has consigned them to:

I also am a daughter of the colony.
I share their broken speech, their other-whereness.

No testament or craft of mine can hide
our presence
on the distaff side of history.

See: they pull the brims of their hats
down against a gust from the harbour.

They cover
their faces with what should have been
and never quite was: their home.

5 *Imago*

Head of a woman. Half-life of a nation.
Coarsely-cut blackthorn walking stick.
Old Tara brooch.
And bog oak.
A harp and a wolfhound on an ashtray.

All my childhood
I took you for the truth.

I see you now for what you are.

My ruthless images. My simulacra.
Anti-art. A foul skill
traded by history
to show a colony

the way to make pain a souvenir.

6 The Scar

Dawn on the river.
Dublin rises out of what reflects it.

Anna Liffey
looks to the east, to the sea,
her profile carved out by the light
on the old Carlisle bridge.

I was five
when a piece of glass
cut my head and left a scar.
Afterwards my skin felt different.

And still does on these autumn days when
the mist hides the city
from the Liffey.

The Liffey hides
the long ships, the muskets and the burning domes.

Everything but this momentary place.
And those versions of the Irish rain
which change the features
of a granite face.

If colony is a wound what will heal it?
After such injuries
what difference do we feel?

No answer in the air,
on the water, in the distance.
And yet

Emblem of this old,
torn and traded city,
altered by its river, its weather,
I turn to you as if there were.

One flawed head towards another.

7 *City of Shadows*

When I saw my father
buttoning his coat at Front Gate
I thought he would look like a man
who had lost what he had. And he did.

Grafton Street and Nassau Street were gone.
And the old parliament at College Green.
And the bronze arms and attitudes of orators
from Grattan to O'Connell. All gone.

We went to his car. He got in.
I waved my hands and motioned him to turn
his wheel towards the road to the only
straight route out to the coast.

When he did
I walked beside the car,
beside the kerb, and we made our way
in dark inches to the Irish Sea.

Then I smelled salt
and heard the foghorn.
And realised suddenly that I
had brought my father to his destination.

I walked home
alone to my flat.
The fog was lifting slowly. I thought
whatever the dawn made clear

and cast-iron and adamant again,
I would know from now on that in
a lost land of orators and pedestals
and corners and street names and rivers,

where even the ground underfoot
was hidden from view, there had been
one way out.
And I found it.

8 Unheroic

It was an Irish summer. It was wet.
It was a job. I was seventeen.
I set the clock and caught the bus at eight
and leaned my head against the misty window.
The city passed by. I got off
above the Liffey on a street of statues:
iron orators and granite patriots.
Arms wide. Lips apart. Last words.

I worked in a hotel. I carried trays.
I carried keys. I saw the rooms
when they were used and airless and again
when they were aired and ready and I stood
above the road and stared down at
silent eloquence and wet umbrellas.

There was a man who lived in the hotel.
He was a manager. I rarely saw him.
There was a rumour that he had a wound
from war or illness – no one seemed sure –
which would not heal. And when he finished
his day of ledgers and telephones he went
up the back stairs to his room
to dress it. I never found out
where it was. Someone said in his thigh.
Someone else said deep in his side.

He was a quiet man. He spoke softly.
I saw him once or twice on the stairs
at the back of the building by the laundry.
Once I waited, curious to see him.

Mostly I went home. I got my coat
and walked bare-headed to the river
past the wet, bronze and unbroken skin
of those who learned their time and knew their country.

How do I know my country? Let me tell you
it has been hard to do. And when I do
go back to difficult knowledge, it is not
to that street or those men raised
high above the certainties they stood on –
Ireland hero history – but how

I went behind the linen room and up
the stone stairs and climbed to the top.
And stood for a moment there, concealed
by shadows. In a hiding place.
Waiting to see.
Wanting to look again.
Into the patient face of the unhealed.

9 The Colonists

I am ready to go home
through an autumn evening.

Suddenly,
without any warning, I can see them.

They form slowly out of the twilight.
Their faces. Arms. Greatcoats. And tears.

They are holding maps.
But the pages are made of failing daylight.
Their tears, made of dusk, fall across the names.

Although they know by heart
every inch and twist of the river
which runs through this town, and their houses –
every aspect of the light their windows found –
they cannot find where they come from:

The river is still there.
But not their town.
The light is there. But not their moment in it.
Nor their memories. Nor the signs of life they made.

Then they faded.
And the truth is I never saw them.
If I had I would have driven home
through an ordinary evening, knowing
that not one street name or sign or neighbourhood

could be trusted
to the safe-keeping
of the making and unmaking of a people.

And have entered a house I might never
find again, and have written down –
as I do now –

their human pain. Their ghostly weeping.

10 *A Dream of Colony*

I dreamed we came to an iron gate.
And leaned against it.

It opened.
We heard it grinding slowly over gravel.

We began to walk.
When we started talking
I saw our words had the rare power
to unmake history:

Gradually the elms beside us
shook themselves into leaves.
And laid out under us their undiseased shadows.

Each phrase of ours,
holding still for a moment in the stormy air,
raised an unburned house
at the end of an avenue of elder and willow.

Unturned that corner
the assassin eased around and aimed from.
Undid. Unsaid:
Once. Fire. Quick. Over there.

The scarred granite healed in my sleep.
The thundery air became sweet again.
We had come to the top of the avenue.

I heard laughter and forgotten consonants.
I saw greatcoats and epaulettes.
I turned to you –

but who are you?

Before I woke I heard a woman's voice cry out.
It was hoarse with doubt.
She was saying,
I was saying –

What have we done?

11 *A Habitable Grief*

Long ago
I was a child in a strange country:

I was Irish in England.

I learned
a second language there
which has stood me in good stead –

the lingua franca of a lost land.

A dialect in which
what had never been could still be found.

That infinite horizon. Always far
and impossible. That contrary passion
to be whole.

This is what language is:
a habitable grief. A turn of speech
for the everyday and ordinary abrasion
of losses such as this

which hurts
just enough to be a scar.

And heals just enough to be a nation.

12 The Mother Tongue

The old pale ditch can still be seen
less than half a mile from my house –

its ancient barrier of mud and brambles
which mireth next unto Irishmen
is now a mere rise of coarse grass,
a rowan tree and some thinned-out spruce,
where a child is playing at twilight.

I stand in the shadows. I find it
hard to believe now that once
this was a source of our division:

Dug. Drained. Shored up and left
to keep out and keep in. That here
the essence of a colony's defence
was the substance of the quarrel with its purpose:

Land. Ground. A line drawn in rain
and clay and the roots of wild broom –
behind it the makings of a city,
beyond it rumours of a nation –
by Dalkey and Kilternan and Balally
through two ways of saying their names.

A window is suddenly yellow.
A woman is calling a child.
She turns from her play and runs to her name.

Who came here under cover of darkness
from Glenmalure and the Wicklow hills
to the limits of this boundary? Who whispered
the old names for love to this earth
and anger and ownership as it opened
the abyss of their future at their feet?

I was born on this side of the Pale.
I speak with the forked tongue of colony.
But I stand in the first dark and frost
of a winter night in Dublin and imagine

my pure sound, my undivided speech
travelling to the edge of this silence.
As if to find me. And I listen: I hear
what I am safe from. What I have lost.

II The Lost Land

The Lost Land

I have two daughters.

They are all I ever wanted from the earth.
Or almost all.

I also wanted one piece of ground.

One city trapped by hills. One urban river.
An island in its element.

So I could say *mine. My own.*
And mean it.

Now they are grown up and far away

and memory itself
has become an emigrant,
wandering in a place
where love dissembles itself as landscape.

Where the hills
are the colours of a child's eyes,
where my children are distances, horizons.

At night,
on the edge of sleep,
I can see the shore of Dublin Bay,
its rocky sweep and its granite pier.

Is this, I say
how they must have seen it,
backing out on the mailboat at twilight,

shadows falling
on everything they had to leave?
And would love forever?
And then

I imagine myself
at the landward rail of that boat
searching for the last sight of a hand.

I see myself
on the underworld side of that water,
the darkness coming in fast, saying
all the names I know for a lost land.

Ireland. Absence. Daughter.

Mother Ireland

At first
   I was land
        I lay on my back to be fields
and when I turned
      on my side
           I was a hill
under freezing stars.
     I did not see.
         I was seen.
Night and day
     words fell on me.
             Seeds. Raindrops.

Chips of frost.
    From one of them
            I learned my name.
                                    I rose up. I remembered it.
Now I could tell my story.
    It was different
            from the story told about me.
And now also
    it was spring.
            I could see the wound I had left
in the land by leaving it.
            I travelled west.
                            Once there
    I looked with so much love
            at every field
as it unfolded
            its rusted wheel and its pram chassis
                            and at the gorse-
bright distances
    I had been
            that they misunderstood me.
        Come back to us
    they said.
            Trust me I whispered.

The Blossom

A May morning.
Light starting in the sky.

I have come here
after a long night.
Its senses of loss.
Its unrelenting memories of happiness.

The blossom on the apple tree is still in shadow,
its petals half-white and filled with water at the core,
in which the freshness and secrecy of dawn are stored
even in the dark.

How much longer
will I see girlhood in my daughter?

In other seasons
I knew every leaf on this tree.
Now I stand here
almost without seeing them

and so lost in grief
I hardly notice what is happening
as the light increases and the blossom speaks,
and turns to me
with blonde hair and my eyebrows and says –

imagine if I stayed here,
even for the sake of your love,
what would happen to the summer?
To the fruit?

Then holds out a dawn-soaked hand to me,
whose fingers I counted at birth
years ago.

And touches mine for the last time.

And falls to earth.

Tree of Life

A tree on a moonless night
has no sap or colour.

It has no flower and no fruit.

It waits for the sun to find them.

I cannot find you
in this dark hour
dear child.

Wait
for dawn to make us clear to one another.

Let the sun
inch above the roof-tops,

Let love
be the light that shows again

the blossom to the root.

*Commissioned by the National Maternity Hospital, Dublin, during its 1994
Centenary, to mark a service to commemorate the babies who had died there.*

The Necessity for Irony

On Sundays,
when the rain held off,
after lunch or later,
I would go with my twelve-year-old
daughter into town,
and put down the time
at junk sales, antique fairs.

There I would
lean over tables,
absorbed by
lace, wooden frames,
glass. My daughter stood
at the other end of the room,
her flame-coloured hair
obvious whenever –
which was not often –

I turned around.
I turned around.
She was gone.
Grown. No longer ready
to come with me, whenever
a dry Sunday
held out its promises
of small histories. Endings.

When I was young
I studied styles: their use
and origin. Which age
was known for which
ornament and was always drawn
to a lyric speech, a civil tone.
But never thought
I would have the need,
as I do now, for a darker one.

Spirit of irony,
my caustic author
of the past, of memory –
and of its pain, which returns
hurts, stings – reproach me now,
remind me
that I was in those rooms,
with my child,
with my back turned to her,
searching – oh irony! –
for beautiful things.

Heroic

Sex and history. And skin and bone.
And the oppression of Sunday afternoon.
Bells called the faithful to devotion.

I was still at school and on my own.
And walked and walked and sheltered from the rain.

The patriot was made of drenched stone.
His lips were still speaking. The gun
he held had just killed someone.

I looked up. And looked at him again.
He stared past me without recognition.

I moved my lips and wondered how the rain
would taste if my tongue were made of stone.
And wished it was. And whispered so that no one
could hear it but him. *Make me a heroine.*

Whose?

Beautiful land the patriot said
and rinsed it with his blood. And the sun rose.
And the river burned. The earth leaned
towards him. Shadows grew long. Ran red.

Beautiful land I whispered. But the roads
stayed put. Stars froze over the suburb.
Shadows iced up. Nothing moved.
Except my hand across the page. And these words.

from CODE

2001

I Marriage

I   In Which Hester Bateman, Eighteenth-Century English Silversmith, Takes an Irish Commission

Hester Bateman made a marriage spoon
And then subjected it to violence.
Chased, beat it. Scarred it and marked it.
All in the spirit of our darkest century:

Far away from grapeshot and tar caps
And the hedge schools and the music of sedition
She is oblivious to she pours out
And lets cool the sweet colonial metal.

Here in miniature a man and woman
Emerge beside each other from the earth,
From the deep mine, from the seams of rock
Which made inevitable her craft of hurt.

They stand side by side on the handle.
She writes their names in the smooth
Mimicry of a lake the ladle is making, in
A flowing script with a moon drowned in it.

Art and marriage: now a made match.
The silver bends and shines and in its own
Mineral curve an age-old tension
Inches towards the light. See how

Past and future and the space between
The semblance of empire, the promise of nation,
Are vanishing in this mediation
Between oppression and love's remembrance

Until resistance is their only element. It is
What they embody, bound now and always.
History frowns on them, yet in its gaze
They join their injured hands and make their vows.

II   *Against Love Poetry*

We were married in summer, thirty years ago. I have loved you
deeply from that moment to this. I have loved other things as well.
Among them the idea of women's freedom. Why do I put these
words side by side? Because I am a woman. Because marriage is not
freedom. Therefore, every word here is written against love poetry.
Love poetry can do no justice to this. Here, instead, is a remembered
story from a faraway history: A great king lost a war and was paraded
in chains through the city of his enemy. They taunted him. They
brought his wife and children to him – he showed no emotion. They
brought his former courtiers – he showed no emotion. They brought
his old servant – only then did he break down and weep. I did not
find my womanhood in the servitudes of custom. But I saw my
humanity look back at me there. It is to mark the contradictions of
a daily love that I have written this. Against love poetry.

III The Pinhole Camera

solar eclipse, August 1999

This is the day
　　and in preparation
　　　　you punch a hole
in a piece of card.
　　　　You hold it up against
a sheet of paper –
　　　　the simplest form
　　of a pinhole camera –
　　　　　　and put the sun
on your right shoulder:
　　　　　　A bright disc
appears on your page.
　　It loses half its diameter.
　　　　And more than half
　　in another minute.
　　　　　　You know
　　the reason for the red berries
darkening, and the road outside
　　　　　darkening, but did you know
　　　　　　that the wedding
　　　　of light and gravity
　　　　　　is forever?
The sun is in eclipse:
　　　　　if this were legend
the king of light would turn his face away.
　　　　　　A single shadow
　　would kill the salmon-rich
rivers and birdlife
　　　　and lilac of this island.
　　　　　　But this is real –
　　how your page records
　　the alignment of planets:
　　　　their governance.
　　　　　　In other words,

the not-to-be-seen-again
                    mystery of
a mutual influence:
                    The motorways
are flowing north.
The sycamores are a perfect green.
                    The wild jasmine
is a speaking white.
          The sun is coming back. As
                    it will. As it must.
                         You track its progress.
I stand and watch.
                    For you and I
such science holds no secrets:
          We are married thirty years,
                    woman and man.
                         Long enough
to know about power and nature.
                    Long enough
          to know which is which.

IV   *Quarantine*

In the worst hour of the worst season
     of the worst year of a whole people
a man set out from the workhouse with his wife.
He was walking – they were both walking – north.

She was sick with famine fever and could not keep up.
     He lifted her and put her on his back.
He walked like that west and west and north.
Until at nightfall under freezing stars they arrived.

In the morning they were both found dead.
    Of cold. Of hunger. Of the toxins of a whole history.
But her feet were held against his breastbone.
The last heat of his flesh was his last gift to her.

Let no love poem ever come to this threshold.
    There is no place here for the inexact
praise of the easy graces and sensuality of the body.
There is only time for this merciless inventory:

Their death together in the winter of 1847.
    Also what they suffered. How they lived.
And what there is between a man and woman.
And in which darkness it can best be proved.

V Embers

One night in winter when a bitter frost
made the whin-paths crack underfoot,
a wretched woman, eyes staring, hair in disarray,
came to the place where the Fianna had pitched camp.

Your face is made of shadow. You are reading.
There is heat from the fire still. I am reading:

She asked every one of them in turn
to take her to his bed, to shelter her with his body.
Each one looked at her – she was old beyond her years.
Each one refused her, each spurned her, except Diarmuid.

When he woke in the morning she was young and beautiful.
And she was his, forever, but on one condition.
He could not say that she had once been old and haggard.
He could not say that she had ever … here I look up.

You are turned away. You have no interest in this.

I made this fire from the first peat of winter.
Look at me in the last, burnished light of it.
Tell me that you feel the warmth still.
Tell me you will never speak about the ashes.

VI   Then

Where are the lives we lived
when we were young?
Our kisses, the heat of our skin, our bitter words?
The first waking to the first child's cry?

VII   First Year

It was our first home –
our damp, upstairs,
one-year eyrie –
above a tree-lined area
nearer the city.

My talkative, unsure,
unsettled self
was everywhere;
but you
were the clear spirit of somewhere.

At night
when we settled down
in the big bed by the window,
over the streetlight
and the first crackle of spring

eased the iron at
the base of the railings,
unpacking crocuses,
it was
the awkward corners of your snowy town

which filled
the rooms we made
and stayed there all year with
the burnt-orange lampshade,
the wasps in the attic.

Where is the soul of a marriage?

Because I am writing this
not to recall our lives,
but to imagine them,
I will say it is
in the first gifts of place:

the steep inclines
and country silences
of your boyhood,
the orange-faced narcissi
and the whole length of the Blackwater

strengthening our embrace.

VIII Once

The lovers in an Irish story never had good fortune.
They fled the king's anger. They lay on the forest floor.
They kissed at the edge of death.

Did you know our suburb was a forest?
Our roof was a home for thrushes.
Our front door was a wild shadow of spruce.

Our faces edged in mountain freshness,
we took our milk in where the wide apart
prints of the wild and never-seen
creatures were set who have long since died out.

I do not want us to be immortal or unlucky.
To listen for our own death in the distance.
Take my hand. Stand by the window.

I want to show you what is hidden in
this ordinary, ageing human love is
there still and will be until

an inland coast so densely wooded
not even the ocean fog could enter it
appears in front of us and the chilled-
to-the-bone light clears and shows us

Irish wolves. A silvery man and wife.
Yellow-eyed. Edged in dateless moonlight.
They are mated for life. They are legendary. They are safe.

IX   *Thankëd be Fortune*

Did we live a double life?
> I would have said
> > we never envied
the epic glory of the star-crossed.
> I would have said
> > we learned by heart
the code marriage makes of passion –
> > *duty dailyness routine.*
But after dark when we went to bed
under the bitter fire
> > of constellations,
> orderly, uninterested and cold –
> > at least in our case –
in the bookshelves just above our heads,
> all through the hours of darkness,
> > men and women
wept, cursed, kept and broke faith
> and killed themselves for love.
> > Then it was dawn again.
Restored to ourselves,
> we woke early and lay together
listening to our child crying, as if to birdsong,
> with ice on the windowsills
> > and the grass eking out
> the last crooked hour of starlight.

X A Marriage for the Millennium

Do you believe
that Progress is a woman?
A spirit seeking for its opposite?
For a true marriage to ease her quick heartbeat?

I asked you this
as you sat with your glass of red wine
and your newspaper of yesterday's events.
You were drinking and reading, and did not hear me.

Then I closed the door
and left the house behind me and began
driving the whole distance of our marriage,
away from the suburb towards the city.

One by one
the glowing windows went out.
Television screens cooled down more slowly.
Ceramic turned to glass, circuits to transistors.

Old rowans were saplings.
Roads were no longer wide.
Children disappeared from their beds.
Wives, without warning, suddenly became children.

Computer games became codes again.
The codes were folded
back into the futures of their makers.
Their makers woke from sleep, weeping for milk.

When I came to the street we once lived on
with its iron edges out of another century
I stayed there only a few minutes.
Then I was in the car, driving again.

I was ready to tell you when I got home
that high above that street in a room
above the laid-out hedges and wild lilac
nothing had changed

them, nothing ever would.
The man with his creased copy of the newspaper.
Or the young woman talking to him. Talking to him.
Her heart eased by this.

XI   Lines for a Thirtieth Wedding Anniversary

Somewhere up in the eaves it began.
High in the roof – in a sort of vault
between the slates and gutter – a small leak.
Through it, rain which came from the east,
in from the lights and foghorns of the coast,
water with a ghost of ocean salt in it,
spilled down on the path below
over and over and over years
stone began to alter,
its grain searched out, worn in:
granite rounding down, giving way
taking into its own inertia that
information water brought – of ships,
wings, fog and phosphor in the harbour.
It happened under our lives, the rain,
the stone. We hardly noticed. Now
this is the day to think of it, to wonder.
All those years, all those years together –
the stars in a frozen arc overhead,
the quick noise of a thaw in the air,
the blue stare of the hills – through it all
this constancy: what wears, what endures.

II Code

Code

An Ode to Grace Murray Hopper 1906–88
maker of a computer compiler and verifier of COBOL

Poet to poet. I imagine you
  at the edge of language, at the start of summer
    in Wolfeboro New Hampshire, writing code.
      You have no sense of time. No sense of minutes even.
        They cannot reach inside your world,
          your grey workstation,
            with *when yet now never* and *once*.
              You have missed the other seven.
                This is the eighth day of creation.

The peacock has been made, the rivers stocked.
The rainbow has leaned down to clothe the trout.
The earth has found its pole, the moon its tides.
Atoms, energies have done their work,
have made the world, have finished it, have rested.
And we call this Creation. And you missed it.

The line of my horizon, solid blue
  appears at last fifty years away
    from your fastidious, exact patience:
      The first sign that night will be day
        is a stir of leaves in this Dublin suburb
          and air and invertebrates and birds,
            as the earth resorts again
              to its explanations:
                Its shadows. Its reflections. Its words.

You are west of me and in the past.
Dark falls. Light is somewhere else.
The fireflies come out above the lake.
You are compiling binaries and zeroes.
The given world is what you can translate.
And you divide the lesser from the greater.

Let there be language –
   even if we use it differently:
      I never made it timeless as you have.
         I never made it numerate as you did.
            And yet I use it here to imagine
               how at your desk in the twilight
                  legend, history and myth of course,
                     are gathering in Wolfeboro New Hampshire,
                        as if to a memory. As if to a source.

Maker of the future, if the past
is fading from view with the light
outside your window and the single file
of elements and animals, and all the facts
of origin and outcome, which will never find
their way to you or shelter in your syntax –

it makes no difference:
   We are still human. There is still light
      in my suburb and you are in my mind –
         head bowed, old enough to be my mother –
            writing code before the daylight goes.
         I am writing at a screen as blue
            as any hill, as any lake, composing this
               to show you how the world begins again:
                  One word at a time.
                     One woman to another.

Limits

So high
in their leafy silence
over Kells, over Durrow
as the Vikings
raged south –
the old monks
made the alphabet
wild:
          they dipped iron
into azure and
indigo: they gave strange
wings to their o's
and e's: their vowels
clung on with
talons and the thin,
ribbed wolves
which had gone north
left their frozen winters
and were lured back
to their consonants.

Limits 2

If there was
a narrative to my life
in those years, then
let this
be the sound of it –
the season in, season out
sound of
the grind of
my neighbours' shears.

Beautiful air of August,
music of limitation, of
the clipped
shadow and
the straightened border,
of rain on the Dublin hills,
of my children sleeping in
a simpler world:
an iron edge
the origin of order.

How We Made a New Art on Old Ground

A famous battle happened in this valley.
        You never understood the nature poem.
Till now. Till this moment – if these statements
        seem separate, unrelated, follow this

silence to its edge and you will hear
        the history of air: the crispness of a fern
or the upward cut and turn around of
        a fieldfare or thrush written on it.

The other history is silent: the estuary
        is over there. The issue was decided here:
Two kings prepared to give no quarter.
        Then one king and one dead tradition.

Now the humid dusk, the old wounds
        wait for language, for a different truth:
When you see the silk of the willow
        and the wider edge of the river turn

and grow dark and then darker, then
                    you will know that the nature poem
is not the action nor its end: it is
                    this rust on the gate beside the trees, on

the cattle grid underneath our feet,
                    on the steering wheel shaft: it is
an aftermath, an overlay and even in
                    its own modest way, an art of peace:

I try the word *distance* and it fills with
                    sycamores, a summer's worth of pollen.
And as I write *valley* straw, metal
                    blood, oaths, armour are unwritten.

Silence spreads slowly from these words
                    to those ilex trees half in, half out
of shadows falling on the shallow ford
                    of the south bank beside Yellow Island

as twilight shows how this sweet corrosion
                    begins to be complete: what we see
is what the poem says:
                    evening coming – cattle, cattle-shadows –

and whin bushes and a change of weather
                    about to change them all: what we see is how
the place and the torment of the place are
                    for this moment free of one another.

Making Money

At the turn of the century, the paper produced there was of such high quality that it was exported for use as bank-note paper.

'Dundrum and its Environs'

They made money –
                              maybe not the way
you think it should be done
but they did it anyway.

At the end of summer
the rains came and braided
the river Slang as it ran down and down
the Dublin mountains and into faster water
and stiller air as if a storm was coming in.
And the mill wheel turned so the mill
could make paper and the paper money.
And the cottage doors opened and the women
came out in the ugly first hour
after dawn and began

                              to cook the rags they put
hemp waste, cotton lint, linen, flax and fishnets
from boxes delivered every day on
the rag wagon on a rolling boil. And the steam rose
up from the open coils where a shoal slipped through
in an April dawn. And in the backwash they added
alkaline and caustic and soda ash and suddenly
they were making money.

                              A hundred years ago
this is the way they came to the plum-brown
headlong weir and the sedge drowned in it
and their faces about to be as they looked down
once quickly on
their way to the mill, to the toil
of sifting and beating and settling and fraying

the weighed-out fibres. And they see how easily
the hemp has forgotten the Irish sea at
neap tide and how smooth the weave is now in
their hands. And they do not and they never will

see the small boundaries all this will buy
or the poisoned kingdom with its waterways
and splintered locks or the peacocks who will walk
this paper up and down in the windless gardens
of a history no one can stop happening now.
Nor the crimson and indigo features
of the prince who will stare out from
the surfaces they have made on
the ruin of a Europe
he cannot see from the surface
of a wealth he cannot keep
                              if you can keep
your composure in the face of this final proof that
the past is not made out of time, out of memory,
out of irony but is also
a crime we cannot admit and will not atone
it will be dawn again in the rainy autumn of the year.
The air will be a skinful of water –
the distance between storms –
again. The wagon of rags will arrive.
The foreman will buy it. The boxes will be lowered to the path
the women are walking up
as they always did, as they always will now.
Facing the paradox. Learning to die of it.

Exile! Exile!

All night the room breathes out its grief.
Exhales through surfaces. The sideboard.
The curtains. The stale air stalled there.
The kiln-fired claws of the china bird.

This is the hour when every ornament
unloads its atoms of pretence. Stone.
Brass. Bronze. What they represent is
set aside in the dark. They become again

a spacious morning in the Comeraghs.
An iron gate; a sudden downpour; a well in
the corner of a farmyard; a pool of rain
into which an Irish world has fallen.

Out there the Americas stretch to the horizons.
They burn in the cities and darken over wheat.
They go to the edge, to the rock, to the coast,
to where the moon abrades a shabby path eastward.

O land of opportunity, you are
not the suppers with meat, nor
the curtains with lace nor the unheard of
fire in the grate on summer afternoons, you are

this room, this dish of fruit which
has never seen its own earth. Or had rain
fall on it all one night and the next. And has grown,
in consequence, a fine, crazed skin of porcelain.

Is It Still the Same

young woman who climbs the stairs,
who closes a child's door,
who goes to her table
in a room at the back of a house?
The same unlighted corridor?
The same night air
over the wheelbarrows and rain-tanks?
The same inky sky and pin-bright stars?
You can see nothing of her, but her head
bent over the page, her hand moving,
moving again, and her hair.
I wrote like that once.
But this is different.
This time, when she looks up, I will be there.

Irish Poetry

for Michael Hartnett

We always knew there was no Orpheus in Ireland.
No music stored at the doors of hell.
No god to make it.
No wild beasts to weep and lie down to it.

But I remember an evening when the sky
was underworld-dark at four,
when ice had seized every part of the city
and we sat talking –
the air making a wreath for our cups of tea.

And you began to speak of our own gods.
Our heartbroken pantheon.

No Attic light for them and no Herodotus.
But thin rain and dogfish and the stopgap
of the sharp cliffs
they spent their winters on.

And the pitch-black Atlantic night.
How the sound
of a bird's wing in a lost language sounded.

You made the noise for me.
Made it again.
Until I could see the flight of it: suddenly

the silvery lithe rivers of the south-west
lay down in silence
and the savage acres no one could predict
were all at ease, soothed and quiet and
listening to you, as I was. As if to music, as if to peace.

from DOMESTIC VIOLENCE

2007

Domestic Violence

1 Domestic Violence

1

It was winter, lunar, wet. At dusk
pewter seedlings became moonlight orphans.
Pleased to meet you meat to please you
said the butcher's sign in the window in the village.

Everything changed the year that we got married.
And after that we moved out to the suburbs.
How young we were, how ignorant, how ready
to think the only history was our own.

And there was a couple who quarrelled into the night,
their voices high, sharp:
nothing is ever entirely
right in the lives of those who love each other.

2

In that season suddenly our island
broke out its old sores for all to see.
We saw them too.
We stood there wondering how

the salt horizons and the Dublin hills,
the rivers, table mountains, Viking marshes
we thought we knew
had been made to shiver

into our ancient twelve by fifteen television
which gave them back as grey and greyer tears
and killings, killings, killings,
then moonlight-coloured funerals:

nothing we said
not then, not later,
fathomed what it is
is wrong in the lives of those who hate each other.

3

And if the provenance of memory is
only that – remember, not atone –
and if I can be safe in
the weak spring light in that kitchen, then

why is there another kitchen, spring light
always darkening in it and
a woman whispering to a man
over and over *what else could we have done?*

4

We failed our moment or our moment failed us.
The times were grand in size and we were small.
Why do I write that
when I don't believe it?

We lived our lives, were happy, stayed as one.
Children were born and raised here
and are gone,
including ours.

As for that couple did we ever
find out who they were
and did we want to?
I think we know. I think we always knew.

2 How the Dance Came to the City

It came with the osprey, the cormorants, the air
at the edge of the storm, on the same route as
the blight and with the nightly sweats that said *fever*.

It came with the scarlet tunics and rowel-spurs,
with the epaulettes and their poisonous drizzle of gold,
with the boots, the gloves, the whips, the flash of the cuirasses.

It came with a sail riding the empire-blue haze
of the horizon growing closer, gaining and then
it was there: the whole creaking orchestra of salt and canvas.

And here is the cargo, deep in the hold of the ship,
stored with the coiled ropes and crated spice and coal,
the lumber and boredom of arrival, underneath

timbers shifting and clicking from the turnaround
of the tides locked at the mouth of Dublin Bay, is
the two-step, the quick step, the whirl, the slow return.

Tonight in rooms where skirts appear steeped in tea
when they are only deep in shadow and where heat
collects at the waist, the wrist, is wet at the base of the neck,

the secrets of the dark will be the truths of the body
a young girl feels and hides even from herself as she lets fall
satin from her thighs to her ankles, as she lets herself think

how it started, just where: with the minuet, the quadrille,
the chandeliers glinting, the noise wild silk makes and
her face flushed and wide-eyed in the mirror of his sword.

3 How It Was Once In Our Country

In those years I owned a blue plate,
blue from the very edges to the centre,
ocean-blue, the sort of under-wave blue
a mermaid could easily dive down into and enter.

When I looked at the plate I saw the mouth
of a harbour, an afternoon without a breath
of air, the evening clear all the way to Howth
and back, the sky a paler blue further to the south.

Consider the kind of body that enters blueness,
made out of dead-end myth and mischievous
whispers of an old, borderless
existence where the body's meaning is both more and less.

Sea-trawler, land-siren: succubus to all the dreams
land has of ocean, of its old home.
She must have witnessed deaths. Of course she did.
Some say she stayed down there to escape the screams.

4 Still Life

William Harnett was a famous realist.

He went from Clonakilty to Philadelphia
in the aftermath of Famine. In

the same year the *London Illustrated News*
printed an etching of a woman.

On one arm was a baby – rigid, still.
In her other hand was a small dish.

They called it *Woman Begging at Clonakilty*.

I believe the surfaces of things
can barely hold in what is under them.

He became a painter.
He painted objects and instruments, household and musical.

He laid them on canvases with surfaces and textures
no light could exit from.

He painted his Cremona violin as if only he knew
the skin tones of spruce wood.

I drove through Clonakilty in early spring
when the air was tinged with a colour close to vinegar,
a sure sign of rain,

past the corn store and the old linen mill,
down Long Quay.

I looked back at fields, at the air extracting
the essence of stillness from the afternoon.

(The child, of course, was dead.)

5 Silenced

In the ancient, gruesome story, Philomel
was little more than an ordinary girl.

She went away with her sister, Procne. Then
her sister's husband, Tereus, given to violence,
raped her once

and said he required her silence
forever. When she whispered *but*
he finished it all and had her tongue cut out.

Afterwards, she determined to tell her story
another way. She began a tapestry.
She gathered skeins, colours.
She started weaving.

She was weaving alone, in fact, and so intently
she never saw me enter.

An Irish sky was unfolding its wintry colours
slowly over my shoulder. An old radio
was there in the room as well, telling its own
unregarded story of violation.

Now she is rinsing the distances
with greenish silks. Now, for the terrible foreground,
she is pulling out crimson thread.

6 Histories

That was the year the news was always bad
(statistics on the radio)
the sad
truth no less so for being constantly repeated.

That was the year my mother was outside
in the shed
in her apron with the strings tied
twice behind her back and the door left wide.

7 Wisdom

The air hoarded frost. The lilac was a ghost
of lilac. It was eerie and expectant, both.
Metal touched clay, grated against stone. It was all
detailed, slow. Cigarettes were lit, there was laughter.
They were digging up an era, a city, my life.
They were using spades, machines, their wits.
I was standing there watching, on
a dry night in a small town in Ireland.
In this place, archaeology was not a science,
nor a search for the actual, nor a painstaking
catalogue of parts and bone fragments, but
an art of memory and this, I thought, is how
legends have been, and will always be, edited –
not by saying them, but by unsettling
one layer of meaning from another and
another, and now they were pulling up something,
pushing its surface back into the world,
lifting it clear of its first funeral, moonlight
catching it, making it seem as if

it was swimming in and out of those gleams,
promising, disappearing. Then
I saw what it was – a plate, a round utensil,
a common flatness on which was served every day
the sustenance and restitution
of who we were once,
its substance braided with the dust of everything
that had happened since.
There was silence. No one looked up. Or spoke.
And then I knew I needed to tell you something:
The salmon of knowledge was fat and slick,
a sliver of freckles in the shallow water
and sought-after reflections of our old legends.
The hero ate the flesh and was wiser.
I wanted to say that to you. Then I woke.

8 Irish Interior

The woman sits and spins. She makes no sound.
The man behind her stands by the door.
There is always this: a background, a foreground.

This much we know. They do not want to be here.
The year is 1890. The inks have long since dried.
The name of the drawing is *An Irish interior*.

The year is 1890. Before the inks are dry
Parnell will fall and orchards burn where the two
Captains – Moonlight, Boycott – have had their way.

She has a spinning wheel. He has a loom.
She has a shawl. He stands beside a landscape –
maybe a river, maybe hills, maybe even a farm

opening into a distance of water–song and a wood
they cannot reach: nothing belongs to them but this
melody and tyranny and hopelessness of thread

rendered by linework and the skewed perspective
the eye attains between his hand and the way
her hand rests on the wheel which goes to prove

only this: that there is always near and far, as
she works in one. He weaves inside the other.
Which we are in has yet to be made clear as

we stare through the lines until their lives
have almost disappeared and all we see, all
we want to see, are places in the picture light forgives,

such as the grain of the wood and the close seal of
the thread at the top of the loom and a door opening
into an afternoon they can never avail of.

9 In Our Own Country

They are making a new Ireland
at the end of our road,
under our very eyes,
under the arc lamps they aim and beam

into distances where we once lived
into vistas we will never recognise.

We are here to watch.
We are looking for new knowledge.

They have been working here in all weathers
tearing away the road to our village –
bridge, path, river, all
lost under an onslaught of steel.

An old Europe
has come to us as a stranger in our city,
has forgotten its own music, wars and treaties,
is now a machine from the Netherlands or Belgium

dragging, tossing, breaking apart the clay
in which our timid spring used to arrive
with our daffodils in a single, crooked row.

Remember the emigrant boat?
Remember the lost faces burned in the last glances?
The air clearing away to nothing, nothing, nothing.

Construction work is finished for the night.
The barriers are pulled across the walkway.
They hang a sign on them. It reads *no entry*.

We pull our collars tightly round our necks
but the wind finds our throats,
predatory and wintry.

We walk home. What we know is this
(and this is all we know): We are now
and we will always be from now on –
for all I know we have always been –

exiles in our own country.

Letters to the Dead

An Elegy for my Mother In Which She Scarcely Appears

I knew we had to grieve for the animals
a long time ago: weep for them, pity them.
I knew it was our strange human duty
to write their elegies after we arranged their demise.
I was young then and able for the paradox.
I am older now and ready with the question:
What happened to them all? I mean to those
old dumb implements which have
no eyes to plead with us like theirs,
no claim to make on us like theirs? I mean –

there was a singing kettle. I want to know
why no one tagged its neck or ringed the tin
base of its extinct design or crouched to hear
its rising shriek in winter or wrote it down with
the birds in their blue sleeves of air
torn away with the trees that sheltered them.

And there were brass firedogs which lay out
all evening on the grate and in the heat
thrown at them by the last of the peat fire
but no one noted down their history or put them
in the old packs under slate-blue moonlight.
There was a wooden clothes horse, absolutely steady
without sinews, with no mane and no meadows
to canter in; carrying, instead of
landlords or Irish monks, rinsed tea cloths
but still, I would have thought, worth adding to
the catalogue of what we need, what we always need

as is my mother, on this Dublin evening of
fog crystals and frost as she reaches out to test
one corner of a cloth for dryness as the prewar
Irish twilight closes in and down on the room
and the curtains are drawn and here am I,
not even born and already a conservationist,
with nothing to assist me but the last
and most fabulous of beasts – language, language –
which knows, as I do, that it's too late
to record the loss of these things but does so anyway,
and anxiously, in case it shares their fate.

Amber

It never mattered that there was once a vast grieving:

trees on their hillsides, in their groves, weeping –
a plastic gold dropping

through seasons and centuries to the ground –
until now.

On this fine September afternoon from which you are absent
I am holding, as if my hand could store it,
an ornament of amber

you once gave me.

Reason says this:
The dead cannot see the living.
The living will never see the dead again.

The clear air we need to find each other in is
gone forever, yet

this resin once
collected seeds, leaves and even small feathers as it fell
and fell

which now in a sunny atmosphere seem as alive as
they ever were

as though the past could be present and memory itself
a Baltic honey –

a chafing at the edges of the seen, a showing off of just how much
can be kept safe

inside a flawed translucence.

And Soul

My mother died one summer –
the wettest in the records of the state.
Crops rotted in the west.
Checked tablecloths dissolved in back gardens.
Empty deckchairs collected rain.
As I took my way to her
through traffic, through lilacs dripping blackly
behind houses
and on curbsides, to pay her
the last tribute of a daughter, I thought of something
I remembered
I heard once that the body is, or is
said to be, almost all
water and as I turned southward, that ours is
a city of it
one in which
every single day the elements begin

a journey towards each other that will never,
given our weather,
fail –
         the ocean visible in the edges cut by it,
cloud colour reaching into air,
the Liffey storing one and summoning the other,
salt greeting the lack of it at the North Wall and
as if that wasn't enough, all of it
ending up almost every evening
inside our speech –
coast canal ocean river stream and now
mother and I drove on and although
the mind is unreliable in grief at
the next cloudburst it almost seemed
they could be shades of each other,
the way the body is
of every one of them and now
they were on the move again – fog into mist,
mist into sea spray and both into the oily glaze
that lay on the railings of
the house she was dying in
as I went inside.

On This Earth

We walk in sunshine to the Musée Marmottan. There,
on the wall opposite, I want to show you
Julie Manet

wearing her mother's brushstrokes,
clothed in the ochres of decorum, the hot bonnets
and silks of that century.

Hard to believe as we cross the road – the grass
dry, cropped and exhausted – that there was ever
a flood on this earth.

We leave the museum and go to a nearby café.
In the harsh noon light your cheeks are flushed.
The line is not perfect.

My first daughter you were my dove, my summer,
my skies lifting, my waters retreating,
my covenant with the earth.

Letters to the Dead

I

In the Old Kingdom scholars found pottery
written round and around with signs and marks.

II

Written in silt ware. On the rims of bowls.
Laid at the entrance to tombs.
Red with the iron of one world.
Set at the threshold of another.
They called them letters to the dead.

III

They did not mourn or grieve these signs or marks.
They were intimate, imploring, local, desperate.

IV

Here at the threshold of an Irish spring
you can no longer see,
hawthorn bushes with their small ivory flowers
will soon come alive in every wind. Soon,
every hillside will be a distant bride.

V

If I could write it differently,
the secret history of a place,
as if it were a story of hidden water, known only
through the strange acoustic of a stream underfoot
in shallow grass
it would be this –
this story.

VI

I wanted to bring you the gifts of the island,
the hawthorn in the last week of April,
the sight of the Liffey above Leixlip.
The willows there could be girls,
their hair still wet after a swim.
Instead, I have brought you a question.

VII

How many daughters stood alone at a grave,
and thought this of their mothers' lives?
That they were young in a country that hated a woman's body.
That they grew old in a country that hated a woman's body.

VIII

They asked for the counsel of the dead.
They asked for the power of the dead.
These are my letters to the dead.

To Memory

This is for you, goddess that you are.
This is a record for us both, this is a chronicle.
There should be more of them, they should be lyrical
and factual, and true, they should be written down
and spoken out on rainy afternoons, instead of which
they fall away; so I have written this, so it will not.
My last childless winter was the same
as all the other ones. Outside my window
the motherless landscape hoarded its own kind.
Light fattened the shadows; frost harried the snowdrops.
There was a logic to it, the way my mother loved astrology –

she came from a valley in the country
where everything that was haphazard and ill-timed
about our history had happened and so it seemed natural
that what she wanted most were the arts of the pre-determined.
My child was born at the end of winter. How to prove it?
Not the child, of course, who slept in pre-spring darkness,
but the fact that the ocean – moonless, stripped of current –
entered the room quietly one evening and
lay down in the weave of the rug, and could be seen
shifting and sighing in blue-green sisal and I said
nothing about it, then or later, to anyone and when
the spring arrived I was ready to see a single field in
the distance on the Dublin hills allow its heathery colour
to detach itself and come upstairs and settle in
the corner of the room furthest from the window.
I could, of course, continue. I could list for you
a whole inventory of elements and fixed entities
that broke away and found themselves disordered in
that season – assembling, dispersing – and without
a thought for laws that until then had barred
an apple flower from opening out at midnight
or lilac rooting in the coldest part of ocean. Then
it stopped. Little by little what was there came back.
Slowly at first; then surely. I realised what had happened
was secret, hardly possible, to be remembered always,
which is why you are listening as rain comes down,
restored to its logic, responsive to air and land
and I am telling you this: you are after all
not simply the goddess of memory, you have
nine daughters yourself and can understand.

Becoming the Hand of John Speed

Atlantis – A Lost Sonnet

How on earth did it happen, I used to wonder
that a whole city – arches, pillars, colonnades,
not to mention vehicles and animals – had all
one fine day gone under?

I mean, I said to myself, the world was small then.
Surely a great city must have been missed?
I miss our old city –

white pepper, white pudding, you and I meeting
under fanlights and low skies to go home in it. Maybe
what really happened is

this: the old fable-makers searched hard for a word
to convey that what is gone is gone forever and
never found it. And so, in the best traditions of

where we come from, they gave their sorrow a name
and drowned it.

Becoming the Hand of John Speed

How do you make a nation?
How do you make it answer to you?
How do you make its parts, its waterways
its wished-for blueness at the horizon point
take heed?

I have no answer. I was born in a nation
I had no part in making.

But sometimes late at night when I want to imagine
what it was to be a part of it
I take down my book and then I am

the agile mapping hand of John Speed
making *The Kingdome of Ireland, 1612,*

my pen moving over a swerve of contour,
my ink stroke adding an acre of ocean.

The Dublin hills surrender two dimensions.
Forests collapse, flattening all their wolves.

The Irish sea
cedes its ancient tensions,
its gannets, gulls, cormorants all stopped
from flying away by their own silhouettes –

and you might say my nation has become
all but unrecognisable, but no,

I remember the way it was when I was young,
wanting the place to know me at first glance
and it never did,
it never did, and so

this is the way to have it, cut to size,
its waters burned in copper, its air unbreathed
its future neighbourhoods almost all unnamed –

and even the old, ocean-shaped horizon
surprised by its misshapen accuracy –

ready and flat and yearning to be claimed.

Violence Against Women

Once in the West Pennines I was shown
the source of the Industrial Revolution –

the first streams harnessed to the wheels
which drove the mills which spun out textiles

which emptied out the cottages and hillsides
and sent men and women down to Hades.

(Fast water and mountains without lime
and greed all complicit in the shame.)

Real men and women, flesh and blood
and long dead and ready to be understood –

and not those abandoned and unsaved
women who died here who never lived:

Mindless, sexless, birthless, only sunned
by shadows, only dressed in muslin,

shepherdesses of the English pastoral
waiting for the return of an English April

that never came and never will again.
Wheels turned, the jenny worked, a plainspoken

poetry was chanted by the flow
and finished them. They were the last to know

what happened in this north-facing twilight,
the aftermath I saw here, staring at

an old site of injury, a hurt
that never healed and never can. O art,

O empire and the arranged relations,
so often covert, between power and cadence –

tell me what it is you have done with
the satin bonnets and the pastel sun, with

the women gathering their unreal sheep
into real verse for whom no one will weep.

Instructions

To write about age you need to take something and
break it.

(This is an art that has always loved young women.
And silent ones.)

A branch, perhaps, girlish with blossom. Snapped off.
Close to the sap.

Then cut through a promised summer. Continue. Cut
down to the root.

The spring afternoon will come to your door, angry
as any mother. Ignore her.

Now take syntax. Break that too. What is left is for you
and you only:

A dead tree. The future. What does not bear fruit. Or
thinking of.

In Coming Days

Soon
I will be as old as the Shan Van Vocht –

(although no one knows how old she is.)

Soon
I will ask to meet her on the borders of Kildare.

It will be cold.
The hazel willow will be frozen by the wayside.

The rag-taggle of our history
will march by us.

They will hardly notice two women by the roadside.

I will speak to her. Even though I know
she can only speak with words made by others.

I will say to her: You were betrayed.
Do you know that?

She will look past me at the torn banners,
makeshift pikes, bruised feet. Her lips will move:

To the Currach of Kildare
The boys they will repair.

There is still time, I will tell her. We can still
grow old together.

And will Ireland then be free?
And will Ireland then be free?

We loved the same things, I will say –
or at least some of them. Once in fact, long ago -

Yes! Ireland shall be free,
From the centre to the sea -

I almost loved you.

NEW POEMS

Art of Empire

If no one in my family ever spoke of it,
if no one handed down
what it was to be born to power
and married in a poor country.

If no one wanted to remember
the noise of the redcoats cantering
in lanes bleached with apple flowers
on an April morning.

If no one ever mentioned how a woman was,
what she did,
what she never did again,
when she lived in a dying Empire.

If what was not said was never seen
If what was never seen could not be known
think of this as the only way
an empire could recede –

taking its laws, its horses and its lordly all,
leaving a single art to be learned,
and one that required
neither a silversmith nor a glassblower

but a woman skilled in the sort of silence
that lets her stitch shadow flowers
into linen with pastel silks
who never looks up

to remark on or remember why it is
the bird in her blackwork is warning her:
not a word not a word
not a word not a word.

The Long Evenings of their Leavetakings

My mother was married by the water.
She wore a grey coat and a winter rose.

She said her vows beside a cold seam of the Irish coast.

She said her vows near the shore where
the emigrants set down their consonantal *n*:

on after*n*oon, on the e*n*d of everything, at the start of *ever*.

Yellow vestments took in light
a chalice hid underneath its veil.

Her hands were full of calla and cold weather lilies.

The mail packet dropped anchor.
A black headed gull swerved across the harbour.

Icy promises rose beside a cross-hatch of ocean and horizon.

I am waiting for the words of the service. I am waiting for
keep thee only and *all my earthly*.

All I hear is an afternoon's worth of *never*.

Re-reading Oliver Goldsmith's 'Deserted Village' in a Changed Ireland

1

Well not for years – at least not then or then.
I never looked at it. Never took it down.
The place was changing. That much was plain:
Land was sold. The little river was paved over with stone.
Lilac ran wild.
Our neighbours opposite put out the *For Sale* sign.

2

All the while, I let Goldsmith's old lament remain
Where it was: high on my shelves, stacked there at the back –
Dust collecting on its out-of-date,
other-century, superannuated pain.

3

I come from an old country.
Someone said it was past its best. It had missed its time.
But it was beautiful. Blue suggested it, and green defined it.
Everywhere I looked it provided mirrors, mirror flashes, sounds.
Its name was not Ireland. It was Rhyme.

4

I return there for a moment as the days
Wind back, staying long enough to hear vowels rise
Around the name of a place.
Goldsmith's origin but not his source.
Lissoy. Signal and sibilance of a river-hamlet with trees.

And stay another moment to summon his face,
To see his pen work the surface,
To watch lampblack inks laying phrase after phrase
On the island, the village he is taking every possible care to erase.

And then I leave.

Here in our village of Dundrum
The Manor Laundry was once the Corn Mill.
The laundry was shut and became a bowling alley.
The main street held the Petty Sessions and Dispensary.

A spring morning.
A first gleam of sunshine in Mulvey's builder's yard.
The husbands and wives in the walled graveyard
Who brought peace to one another's bodies are not separated.
But wait. Mulvey's hardware closed down years ago.
The cemetery can't be seen from the road.

Now visitors come from the new Town Centre,
Built on the site of an old mill,
Their arms weighed down with brand names, fashion labels, bags.

Hard to know which variant
Of our country this is. Hard to say
Which variant of sound to use at the end of this line.

11

We were strangers here once. Now
Someone else
Is living out their first springtime under these hills.
Someone else
Feels the sudden ease that comes when the wind veers
South and warms rain.
Would any of it come back to us if we gave it another name?
(Sweet Auburn loveliest village of the Plain.)

12

In a spring dusk I walk to the Town Centre,
I stand listening to a small river,
Closed in and weeping.
Everyone leaving in the dusk with a single bag,
The way souls are said to enter the underworld
With one belonging.
And no one remembering.

13

A subject people knows this.
The first loss is through history.
The final one is through language.

14

It is time to go back to where I came from.

15

I take down the book. Centuries and years
Fall softly from the page. Sycamores, monasteries, a schoolhouse
And river-loving trees, their leaves casting iron-coloured shadows,
Are falling and falling
As the small town of Lissoy
Sinks deeper into sweet Augustan double talk and disappears.

As

A squeak of light. Ocean air looking
to come inland, to test its influence on
the salty farms waking.

Mist lifts. The distance
reappears. In an hour or so

someone will say *crystal clear*
even though there is
no truth in it since even now
the ground is clouding its ions and atoms.

The sun is up; day begins.
Someone else says *dry as dust*.
But this is outside Dublin in
summer: last night's storm
left clay and water mixed together.

The afternoon is long and warm.
The branch of one tree angles to
its own heaviness. Everywhere,

everywhere it continues: language crossing
the impossible with
the proverbial –

until no one any longer wants
a world where *as* is not preferred
to its absence. Nor a fiddle not fit,
nor a whistle not clean,
nor rain not right again.

I am walking home. A quarter moon
rises in the whitebeams.
At the next turn houses appear,
mine among them.

I walk past leaves,
grass, one bicycle. I put my key in the lock.

In a little while I will say *safe as*.

Becoming Anne Bradstreet

It happens again
As soon as I take down her book and open it.

I turn the page.
My skies rise higher and hang young stars.

The ship's rail freezes.
Mare Hibernicum leads to Anne Bradstreet's coast.

A blackbird leaves her pine trees
And lands in my spruce trees.

I open my door on a Dublin street.
Her child/her words are staring up at me:

In better dress to trim thee was my mind,
But nought save home-spun cloth, i' th' house I find.

We say *home truths*
Because her words can be at home anywhere –

At the source, at the end and whenever
The book lies open and I am again

An Irish poet watching an English woman
Become an American poet.

Commissioned by the Folger Shakespeare Library
for the exhibition 'Shakespeare's Sisters'.

Cityscape

I have a word for it –
the way the surface waited all day
to be a silvery pause between sky and city –
which is *elver*.

And another one for how
the bay shelved cirrus clouds
piled up at the edge of the Irish Sea,
which is *elver* too.

The old Blackrock baths
have been neglected now for fifty years,
fine cracks in the tiles
visible as they never were when

I can I can I can
shouted Harry Vernon as
he dived from the highest board
curving down into salt and urine

his cry fading out
through the half century it took
to hear as a child that a glass eel
had been seen

entering the sea-water baths at twilight –
also known as *elver* –
and immediately
the word begins

a delicate migration –
a fine crazing healing in the tiles –
the sky deepening above a city
that has always been

unsettled between sluice gates and the Irish Sea
to which there now comes at dusk
a translucent visitor
yearning for the estuary.

A Woman Without a Country

As dawn breaks he enters
A room with the odour of acid.
He lays the copper plate on the table.
And reaches for the shaft of the burin.
Dublin wakes to horses and rain.
Street hawkers call.
All the news is famine and famine.
The flat graver, the round graver
The angle tint tool wait for him.
He bends to his work and begins.
He starts with the head, cutting in
To the line of the cheek, finding
The slope of the skull, incising
The shape of a face that becomes
A foundry of shadows, rendering –
With a deeper cut into copper –
The whole woman as a skeleton,
The rags of her skirt, her wrist
In a bony line forever
                        severing
Her body from its native air until
She is ready for the page,
For the street vendor, for
A new inventory which now
To loss and to *laissez-faire* adds
The odour of acid and the little,
Pitiless tragedy of being imagined.

He puts his tools away,
One by one; lays them out carefully
On the deal table, his work done.

Index of First Lines

A child   40
A famous battle happened in this valley.   189
A May morning   168
A neighbourhood.   128
A squeak of light. Ocean air looking   230
A tree on a moonless night   169
About holiday rooms there can be   124
After a friend has gone I like the feel of it: 72
After the wolves and before the elms   151
Alders are tasselled   96
All night the room breathes out its grief.   193
– and not simply by the fact that this shading of   118
And then the dark fell and 'there has never'   73
As dawn breaks he enters   233
At first   166
At first light the legislator   17
At twilight in   102

Beautiful land the patriot said   172
Bent over   65
Bold as crystal, bright as glass   19
Breakfast over, islanded by noise   43

Ceres went to hell   97
Country hands on the handlebars,   20

Dark falls on this mid-western town   129
Daughters of parsons and of army men.   154
Dawn on the river.   156
Did we live a double life?   183
Do you believe   184
Dressed in the colours of a country day –   5

Easter light in the convent garden   92

Flesh is heretic.   25
From my father's head I sprung   3

Head of a woman. Half-life of a nation.   155
Here is the city –   153
Hester Bateman made a marriage spoon   175

How do you make a nation?   218
How on earth did it happen, I used to wonder   217

I am ready to go home   160
I can imagine if,   112
I decanted them – feather mosses, fan-shaped plants,   67
I dreamed we came to an iron gate.   161
I drove West   99
I found it among curios and silver,   148
I go down step by step.   110
I have a word for it –   233
I have been thinking at random   44
I have two daughters.   165
I have written this   50
I knew we had to grieve for the animals   209
I like this story –   137
I live near the coast. On these summer nights   111
I remember the way the big windows washed   66
I take it down   93
I was standing there   60
I won't go back to it –   59
I wonder about you: whether the blue abrasions   90
'Idle as trout in light Colonel Jones,   12
I've caught you out. You slut. You fat trout.   30
If no one in my family ever spoke of it,   225
If there was   188
In middle age you exchanged the sandals   6
In my last year in College   126
In the ancient, gruesome story, Philomel   204
In the Old Kingdom scholars found pottery   214
In the worst hour of the worst season   178
In those years I owned a blue plate,   202
Intimate as underthings   70
Into this city of largesse   7
is what remained or what they thought   63
It came with the osprey, the cormorants, the air   201
It could be   101
It happens again   231
It is a winter afternoon.   106
It is Easter in the suburb. Clematis   77
It is her eyes   27
It never mattered that there was once a vast grieving: 210
It was a school where all the children wore darned worsted;   82
It was an Irish summer. It was wet.   158

It was early summer. Already 100
It was our first home – 180
It was the first gift he ever gave her 89
It was winter, lunar, wet. At dusk 199

Jean-Baptiste Chardin 57

Life, the story goes, 139
Like oil lamps we put them out the back, 83
Long ago 162
Look. 103

Memory 105
My mother died one summer – 211
My mother was married by the water. 226
My naked face; 28
My window pearls wet. 42

On Sundays, 170
Once in the West Pennines I was shown 219
One night in winter when a bitter frost 179
One summer 40
Our way of life 47

Poet to poet. I imagine you 186

Several things announced the fact to us 4
Sex and history. And skin and bone. 171
She came up the hill carrying water 95
So high 188
Somewhere up in the eaves it began. 185
Soon 221

That was the year the news was always bad 205
The air hoarded frost. The lilac was a ghost 205
The bickering of vowels on the buses, 81
The chimneys have been swept 68
The daffodils are out & how 120
The evening was the same as any other. 146
The first man had flint to spark. He had a wheel 49
The German girls who came to us that winter and 104
The linen map 133
The lovers in an Irish story never had good fortune. 182
The old pale ditch can still be seen 163

The only legend I have ever loved is   130
The radio is playing downstairs in the kitchen.   109
The stilled hub   38
The woman is as round   36
The woman sits and spins. She makes no sound.   206
The women who were singers in the West   117
The wounds are terrible. The paint is old.   123
There are dying arts and   135
There are outsiders, always. These stars –   108
They are making a new Ireland   207
They made money –   191
They stitched blooms from ivory tulle   91
This dry night, nothing unusual   11
This harbour was made by art and force.   152
This is dawn.   35
This is for you, goddess that you are.   215
This is my time: 37
This is St Louis. Where the rivers meet.   121
This is the day   177
This is the hour I love: the in-between,   70
This is the story of a man and woman   78
To write about age you need to take something and   220
Tonight the air smells of cut grass.   132
Town and country at each other's throat –   14
Tryers of firesides,   138

Unpod   52

We always knew there was no Orpheus in Ireland.   194
We walk in sunshine to the Musée Marmottan. There, 213
We were married in summer   176
Well not for years—at least not then or then.   227
When he is ready he is raised and carried   84
When I saw my father   157
When the Peep-O-Day Boys were laying fires down in 119
Where are the lives we lived   180
Where in blind files   21
William Harnett was a famous realist.   202

Yesterday I knew no lullaby   13
You rise, you dawn   45
young woman who climbs the stairs,   194

Index of Titles

A Dream of Colony   161
A False Spring   96
A Habitable Grief   162
A Marriage for the Millennium   184
A Woman Painted on a Leaf   148
A Woman Without a Country   233
After a Childhood Away from Ireland   40
Against Love Poetry   176
Amber   210
An Elegy for my Mother In Which She Scarcely Appears   209
An Irish Childhood in England: 1951   81
An Old Steel Engraving   103
And Soul   211
Anna Liffey   139
Anorexic   25
Art of Empire   225
As   230
Athene's Song   3
Atlantis – A Lost Sonnet   217

Beautiful Speech   126
Becoming Anne Bradstreet   231
Becoming the Hand of John Speed   218
Belfast vs Dublin   7
Bright-Cut Irish Silver   93

Child of Our Time   13
City of Shadows   157
Cityscape   232
Code   186
Cyclist with Cut Branches   20

Daphne Heard with Horror the Addresses of the God   100
'Daphne with her thighs in bark'   50
Daughters of Colony   154
Degas's Laundresses   45
Distances   109
Domestic Interior   36
Domestic Violence   199

Embers   179

Endings	40
Energies	37
Envoi	77
Exile! Exile!	193
Fever	63
First Year	180
Fond Memory	82
From the Painting *Back from Market* by Chardin	5
Heroic	171
Histories	205
How It Was Once In Our Country	202
How the Dance Came to the City	201
How We Made a New Art on Old Ground	189
I Remember	66
Imago	155
In a Bad Light	121
In Coming Days	221
In Exile	104
In Her Own Image	27
In Our Own Country	207
In Which Hester Bateman, Eighteenth-Century English Silversmith, Takes an Irish Commission	175
In Which the Ancient History I Learn Is Not My Own	133
Inscriptions	124
Instructions	220
Irish Interior	206
Irish Poetry	194
Is It Still the Same	194
It's a Woman's World	47
Lace	65
Lava Cameo	137
Legends	138
Letters to the Dead	214
Limits	188
Limits 2	188
Lines for a Thirtieth Wedding Anniversary	185
Listen. This is the Noise of Myth	78
Love	129
Making Money	191
Making Up	28

March 1 1847. By the First Post 120
Midnight Flowers 110
Mise Eire 59
Monotony 38
Mother Ireland 166
Moths 132
My Country in Darkness 151

New Territory 4
Night Feed 35
Nocturne 72

O Fons Bandusiae 19
On This Earth 213
Once 182
Our Origins are in the Sea 111
Outside History 108

Patchwork or the Poet's Craft 44

Quarantine 178

Re-reading Oliver Goldsmith's 'Deserted Village' in a Changed
    Ireland 227

Self-Portrait on a Summer Evening 57
Silenced 204
Song 21
Still Life 202
Suburban Woman 14
Suburban Woman: A Detail 68

Thankëd be Fortune 183
That the Science of Cartography is Limited 118
The Achill Woman 95
The Black Lace Fan My Mother Gave Me 89
The Blossom 168
The Bottle Garden 67
The Briar Rose 70
The Colonists 160
The Death of Reason 119
The Dolls Museum in Dublin 123
The Emigrant Irish 83
The Famine Road 12
The Glass King 84

The Harbour 152
The Journey 73
The Latin Lesson 92
The Laws of Love 17
The Long Evenings of their Leavetakings 226
The Lost Land 165
The Making of an Irish Goddess 97
The Mother Tongue 163
The Muse Mother 42
The Necessity for Irony 170
The New Pastoral 49
The Oral Tradition 60
The Parcel 135
The Photograph on My Father's Desk 101
The Pinhole Camera 177
The Pomegranate 130
The Rooms of Other Women Poets 90
The Scar 156
The Shadow Doll 91
The Singers 117
The War Horse 11
The Woman Turns Herself into a Fish 52
The Women 70
Then 180
This Moment 128
Time and Violence 146
Tirade for the Mimic Muse 30
To Memory 215
Tree of Life 169

Unheroic 158

Violence Against Women 219

We Are Always Too Late 105
We Are Human History. We Are Not Natural History. 102
What Love Intended 112
What We Lost 106
White Hawthorn in the West of Ireland 99
Whose? 172
Wisdom 205
Witness 153
Woman in Kitchen 43

Yeats in Civil War 6